Vital Issues
of the
Hour

IN THE LIGHT OF GOD'S WORD

No. 2

This book has been prepared primarily for group study in connection with the Adult Teacher's Guide available for 75¢ from Regular Baptist Press. However, it is also an excellent and informative book to use for individual instruction and to put into the hands of friends or acquaintances who may be facing these problems in their churches.

Published by

REGULAR BAPTIST PRESS

1800 Oakton Boulevard

Des Plai

CONTENTS

© **Copyright 1976** by Regular Baptist Press. Vol. 25, No. 1. Printed in U.S.A. Dr. Merle R. Hull, Executive Editor; Ruth Herriman, Managing Editor.

CHAPTER 1

Is Patriotism Passé?

by L. DUANE BROWN, PH.D., State Representative, Pennsylvania Association of Regular Baptist Churches

BIBLE PORTION TO READ: Romans 13:1-7

PATRIOTISM is "devotion to one's country." It involves a loyalty and a defense of its precepts and with reference to other countries. It is acclaiming one unique aspect of our American heritage.

The Bible believer must not be caught up in an emotional movement which has no clear basis in the Scriptures. One cult even claims that to salute the flag or to serve in the military is un-Biblical. Others claim that our country has so many earthly problems that one might as well bide his time until Christ returns.

Does the Bible support patriotism? It seems proper for the *American* Christian to support his country with its unique heritage. Some 200 years ago—July 4, 1776—the philosophical basis of our Creator-type of government was penned in the Declaration of Independence. In this document four of God's attributes were stressed. It was not until twelve years later, July 2, 1788, that our present Constitution was adopted.

God is seen as the Source of our right to life, liberty and the pursuit of happiness. Nearly all state constitutions stress the inalienable right to life, liberty and possessions. The Declaration says that governments are "instituted" to protect these rights.

Law, as envisioned by our founding fathers, is the product of divine law. Ideas of right and wrong consequently provide the guide for legislation. The separation of government into three branches was instituted to compensate for man's sinful nature with its historical abuse of power. There was a real concern about social and economic evils even though many of these could not be resolved (such as slavery).

All the great ideas of government and civilization crumble, of course, when the patriotic zeal with its humility before God is not transferred to succeeding generations. America is certainly unique among the modern nations but not indestructible nor divinely established. No promise in God's Word insures America from judgment or annihilation.

What does the Bible say the born-again believer should be in this world, and what should his relationship to his country be? Scriptures which teach directly on this issue are Matthew 22:21; Romans 13:1-7; 1 Peter 2:13-17 and Titus 3:1, 2.

These verses teach that the Bible believer should be patriotic in the right sense. This loyalty requires four vital characteristics: submission, appreciation, intercession and participation.

I. True Patriotism Requires Submission

Human government was established by God following the Noahic Flood. (See Genesis 9:1-7.) The basis of civil government is that man has God-given authority to hold man in account for his actions—even to execute him if he assumes the right to take another's life.

In Romans 13:1-7 the word for "powers" is authorities. The New American Standard Bible reads, "Let every person be in subjection to the governing authorities. For there is no authority except from God, and those which exist are established by God." Remember that when Paul wrote Romans, the wicked Emperor Nero was in authority.

When Paul was in Ephesus, he didn't try to reform that pagan city but to evangelize it! He snatched individuals from sin and Satan, but he did not violate the civil law. (See Acts 19:37.)

Titus 3:1 also teaches submission to civil authority: "Put them in mind to be subject to principalities and powers, to obey magistrates, to be ready to every good work." The outworking of submission involves obeying the laws of the land, paying taxes, sharing responsibility for public defense and showing respect for elected leaders. Jesus gave us the example before Pontius Pilate, and the Apostle Paul did so before the high priest and Roman officials.

Even in Jeremiah's day when captives were taken to Babylon, the most wicked idolatrous city of its day, the Lord commanded the captives: "And seek the peace of the city whither I have caused you to be carried away captives, and pray unto the LORD for it: for in the peace thereof shall ye have peace" (Jer. 29:7).

Should Christians vote and participate in political activities? "Of course!" comes the cry; but the facts are that many do not. A survey taken in Chicago several years ago revealed that 99 percent of the bartenders voted, 97 percent of the gamblers along with their families, but only 29 percent of the Protestant church members voted. Furthermore, only 17 percent of the Protestant ministers voted! Although Christians are pilgrims, they are not gypsies without civil responsibilities.

First Peter 2:13-17 teaches that the Christian's testimony is also involved in good citizenship. Is this not *true* patriotism? Belonging to right-wing political movements, outshouting liberal neighbors and protesting with public marches is not really patriotism by exhibitionism. True patriotism is living a godly life and being active in a Bible-believing church which is evangelizing its community!

II. True Patriotism Is Appreciation

America's heritage is unique. Of all the nations other than Israel, the United States has been signally blessed by God. It was founded on Biblical principles by people searching for freedom and faith as well as fortune. Roger Babson, the well-

4

known economist now deceased, once told of attending a banquet where a South American diplomat was honored. The conversation at the table centered on why North America had prospered but South America with all its resources had remained stagnant and undeveloped. The diplomat resolved the matter with this comment, "In my continent the early settlers came looking for gold, but in North America they came to find God."

No other country was established on the foundation that *God had given* men "inalienable rights" which included life, liberty and the pursuit of happiness. Even though less than 10 percent of the population were evangelical Christians at the time the United States was founded, the people generally believed in the principles of Bible morality, human worth and freedom. This provided the broad base for the political implementation of the Creator-orientated government: "In God We Trust" and "God Bless America." On February 29, 1892 the U.S. Supreme Court ruled unanimously in a case over a church matter, "This is a Christian nation." Traditionally (until recently) Sunday was honored as a day of worship; tax exemptions for churches have been recognized; chaplains are provided in the armed services. Also oaths for public office are taken on the Bible; "In God We Trust" was inscribed on money in defiance of the historical self-centered approach to material goods. Both the national anthem and the pledge of allegiance make reference to God.

History shows the United States had roots in religious convictions long before its independence. The birth of Americanism really came with the Mayflower Compact. The early settlers sought and found God's blessing. Many communities, when driven to establish a local government by necessity of growing numbers, hammered out their laws of order with the aid of the pastor in the local church. Preachers were foremost centers of influence.

The democratic foundation of our early documents originated from Bible convictions. Men like Jefferson, Washington, Madison and others were not all born-again men; but they respected the Scriptures and sought God's direction and protection. Thomas Jefferson especially was influenced by the English philosopher John Locke whose views on soul liberty and human worth came from the Anabaptists.

The colonial Baptists were lovers of freedom and early supporters of the American Revolution. In a letter written after the war to the Baptists, George Washington wrote, "I recollect with satisfaction that the religious society of which you are members have been throughout America, uniformly and almost unanimously, the firm friends to civil liberty and the persevering promoters of our glorious Revolution."

Those men of destiny who led the revolution against English tyranny were men who paid dearly for their love of freedom and devotion to have a "nation under God." Of the fifty-six men who signed the Declaration of Independence, five were captured and tortured by the British; nine fought and died from wounds and hardships of war; twelve had their homes pillaged and burned; two lost their sons in battle; one had two sons captured. Others lost their businesses, homes and fortunes. All were branded as traitors and hounded by the king's troops.

Yet these men pledged their lives, their fortunes and their sacred honor that this nation, under God, would not perish from earth!

What about the countless scores of soldiers and sailors, policemen and firemen and other servants of people who have labored, sacrificed and even died to preserve freedom, safety and dignity for America? Peter has commanded: "Honour all men. Love the brotherhood. Fear God. Honour the king." True patriotism means *appreciation!*

Read Psalm 33:12 and Proverbs 14:34; then think about the statements.

III. True Patriotism Is Intercession

In 1 Timothy 2:1-3 Paul instructed believers that prayer for civil leaders is a primary responsibility—"first of all." The power of prayer plays a mysterious yet marvelous place in the culture, morality and history of any nation. Prayer for America has obviously declined. The rise of wickedness and lawlessness may well be in proportion to the increasing apostasy of Christendom. God's people should come back to God's promise in 2 Chronicles 7:14. (Take time to read it.)

Someone has written that all civilizations followed a nine-point cycle. The steps were as listed:

From *bondage* to *spiritual faith*
From *spiritual faith* to *courage*
From *courage* to *liberty*
From *liberty* to *abundance*
From *abundance* to *selfishness*
From *selfishness* to *complacency*
From *complacency* to *apathy*
From *apathy* to *dependence*
From *dependence* back to *bondage*

7

Professor Richard Hofstader of Columbia University wrote: "We are living in a culture that is secular. Religion does not play the role that it used to play. This is particularly true for people under 40 years of age in this society. When a strong religious bond is missing, there are few things that can hold culture together."

Where is America heading? When its people and leaders, even its churches, forsake the Lord, forget its heritage and indulge in lust, pride and corruption, then anarchy and eventual dictatorship will come. (See Revelation 6:1—19:21.)

The only hope for America is prayer lest deserved judgment fall on her. As Abraham interceded for wicked cities, so believers can prevail with the Lord (James 5:16; Gen. 18:23-33).

IV. True Patriotism Is Participation

How involved should Christians become in their country's affairs? Caution for the believer comes from the Scriptures which teach that the nations of the world are God's program, but they all will turn against Him at the close of this age. (See Psalm 2.) They all will eventually become submissive to Him.

Jesus said, "My kingdom is not of this world" (John 18:36). Oswald Chambers commented: "The great enemy to the Lord Jesus Christ in the present day is the conception of practical work that has not come from the New Testament, but from the systems of the world in which endless energy and activities are insisted upon, but no private life with God."

How true this is! Sincere but ignorant Christians get caught up in the battle of saving America, and

8

they neglect the spiritual warfare for the souls of men! Patriotism—or any activity—which deviates the Christian from loyalty to the local church, evangelism and worldwide missions is not of God.

On the other side, Christians should be good citizens, ideal neighbors and loyal to their country. Those who riot and refuse to support the American traditions claim it violates their conscience. However, the Scriptures, not the conscience, should be the guide for such decisions. The Apostles, when ordered by the governmental officials to cease preaching Christ, said, "We ought to obey God rather than men" (Acts 5:29).

This should be the attitude of believers: We are a heavenly people but with earthly responsibilities.

Prepare To Discuss Intelligently

1. In what stage of the nine-step cycle would you place America today?

2. Be prepared to list three positive ways by which a Christian can express his patriotism.

3. Is there any good reason that a Christian should fail to vote?

CHAPTER 2

Punishment of Wrongdoers

by OSCAR HEGG, D.D., Pastor of Euclid Avenue Baptist Church, Spokane, WA

BIBLE PORTIONS TO READ: Genesis 4:1-26; 6:1-22; Romans 13:1-14

W E LIVE in a very punishment-oriented society," are the introductory words to a recent magazine article featuring Dr. F. B. Skinner, the well-known Yale University psychologist. Although Dr. Skinner reveals an aversion to punishment, believing that there is another method in handling offenses, he does admit to the presence of punishment.

Punishment for wrongdoing is operative in this world although man has not faced his responsibility in performing it. Paul the Apostle has summed up the principle in the words of Galatians 6:7: "For whatsoever a man soweth, that shall he also reap." This axiom of truth is far-reaching, invading all of creation.

I. The Basis for Punishment

Historically the basis for punishment in our society has been man's belief in God—the God Who is Sovereign over the universe, being omnipotent, omniscient and omnipresent—the God Who has revealed Himself as moral, having a standard of right and wrong with punishment for the wrongdoer. This punishment is not based particularly on its being a deterrent to wrongdoing, but rather as the *wage* for wrongdoing. This principle is enlarged upon in a quotation from *Outlines of Theology* by A. H. Hodge (pp. 157, 158). Romans 6:23 bears witness in these words, "For the *wages* of sin is death."

However, today the philosophy of unbelief with its rejection of the living and moral God and the exaltation of man to a supremacy subject to no higher power than himself is demanding a hearing in our land. Such a belief is not new, having always been present; but our intellectual climate and our growing freedom of expression have provided man with liberty to accept or reject the declarations of Scripture. The outlook from this vantage point is softness on punishment, even to the place of dismissing it altogether!

This fact is clearly set forth in a recent book aimed at teachers in the public school:

> We now know that each man creates his own unique world, that he, and he alone generates whatever reality he can ever know. . . . Among other things this means that no man can ever be absolutely certain of anything. The best anyone can ever do is to say how something appears to him. The cosmos offers no absolute confirmation. The "concept of absolute, fixed, unchanging truth, particularly from a polarizing good-bad

11

perspective" is an "out-of-joint concept."[1]

It is obvious, then, that our concept of right and wrong and the punishment of wrongdoers will be determined on the basis of our belief or unbelief in the living God.

Believing that God is and that He alone is the Director of this universe, we must submit to His dictates; and in the realm of punishment we must obey His commands. *Remember* that God rules according to His standard of right and wrong. This includes punishment for wrongdoers!

II. Manifestations of Punishment

A. Observed in Creation

Punishment is seen in the operation of natural law. Violation of these laws have their observable results. To jump off a cliff, expecting a reversal of the law of gravity, in no wise stays off a broken body. Chemists and physicists who disregard the laws operating in their field are subject to disaster. Ignorance in this area does not change the impact of the punishment!

Punishment is also manifest when one tampers with the animal kingdom. To antagonize the "king of the jungle" would be to receive a just recompense of reward.

B. Observed in the Societies of the World

As societies develop, they include regulations and punishments. Even those which fall under the caption of being Communistic, a term which implies deep concern for the common man, have

---

[1]Morris Holman, "Crisis in the Classroom," *True Vine, Fall 1975.*

12

punishment—severe punishment—for all who do not conform to the rules. In fact it is difficult to conceive of a society continuing which does not incorporate into its life a system of punishment for offenders.

It is interesting to note that before the Pilgrims landed on the shores of the new world, they covenanted to be ruled by a document which would control each member of the company.

C. Observed in the Scriptures

Believing that God has spoken and that the Bible is that message, we shouldn't be surprised to find many passages dealing with the subject of punishment.

1. *Punishment Inflicted Directly by God.* Consider the following as examples:

Cain (Gen. 4:11-16). When God made His pronouncement, Cain responded, "My punishment is greater than I can bear." However, it was not mitigated by God!

The Flood (Gen. 6:1—8:22). Rejection of God's warning resulted in the removal of that society. When the door of the ark was shut, there was no change in the announced punishment.

Sarai (Gen. 12:17). In protecting His "chosen," God inflicted punishment on Pharaoh's house although his offense was in ignorance!

Ananias and Sapphira (Acts 5:1-11). As a definite and shocking example of God's righteous indignation toward lying—and that to God—these two met immediate physical death.

Unbelievers (Rom. 6:23; Rev. 20:11-15). In view of history and the demonstrations of God's direct punishment we dare not assume that God will skirt this one. Ponder Hebrews 10:30.

2. *Punishment Administered by Man.* Genesis 9:1-7. Disrespect and destruction of human life were the first offenses to be placed under man's jurisdiction. Capital punishment was to be the consequence of murder. This principle continues throughout Scripture, being affirmed in the New Testament by Christ and the Apostle Paul (Matt. 22:21; Rom. 13:1-14).

Exodus—Deuteronomy. "If we knew, we would do," sums up Israel's appeal to Moses (Deut. 5:27). This prompted God to give the Law, coupled with specific punishments for those who failed to comply. A careful analysis of Scripture will reveal the severity of punishment accompanying the Law (cf. Exod. 21:14; 22:1-8; 35:2; Lev. 18:20-30; 20:2; 24:13, 14; Deut. 6:6-9; 27:15).

III. Responsibility in Punishment

Man's responsibility in punishment is divided between the family, the church and the state. When each is diligent in the task, the entire society functions with a measure of peace and prosperity. Again we need to keep in mind that punishment is first of all for wrongdoing, whether it ever becomes a deterrent to evil.

A. The Family

Being ordained of God, the family stands as a

very important part of God's plan for mankind. Although some sociologists don't accept the family as an absolute, God does. He calls for a man to leave his parents, cleave to his wife and, living together, rear their children according to God's rules (Gen. 2:24; Matt. 19:6).

1. *Children Need To Be Trained.* No child comes into this world programmed to do that which is right (Jer. 17:9; Rom. 3:23). Right actions are the result of right training, beginning the first day and including God's plan of salvation. Life must be directed if it is to develop the kind of character acceptable to God and one that will function in society. In order to accomplish this task there must be a penalty for disobedience (Prov. 22:15; Eph. 6:1-4).

2. *Children Need To Understand Punishment.* Abraham must have been an example of this kind of parenthood (Gen. 18:19). Having made clear to the child the difference between right and wrong, the rewards and penalties must also be clearly presented (Prov. 22:6).

3. *Parents Must Carry Through in Punishment.* Consider Proverbs 13:24 and 23:13, 14. When rules are established and broken, it is the parents' responsibility to administer the punishment. If children don't learn this lesson at home, will they learn it in society? *Note:* If we neglect our responsibility as parents, can we rightfully criticize state officials who have become soft in administering punishment?

B. The Church

It is an established principle in Scripture that all who are born-again believers are to be identified with a local church. In this communion there are certain rules laid down by God, including the discipline of the offenders.

The Guiding Principle (Matt. 18:15-17; 1 Tim. 3:1-16). A church congregation is responsible to maintain a good testimony in the community. This is possible only when each individual member keeps the rules. If sin is allowed to reign and situations are overlooked which scream for correction, the church is failing in its responsibility. Consider carefully Romans 16:17; 1 Corinthians 5:1-13; 2 Thessalonians 3:10-14; Titus 3:10.

C. The State

The state with its rule is ordained of God. It has been authorized to administer punishment on wrongdoers to protect society (Matt. 22:21; Rom. 13:1-14; 1 Pet. 2:13-15). This is a basic principle in the structure of our government.

According to Scripture, governmental officers are just as responsible to God as are gospel ministers. They are commissioned by God to "carry the sword." They are guardians of human life and are to use all means available to maintain decency and order including *capital punishment of those committing deliberately planned murder*.

IV. Growing Softness in Punishment (Ps. 12:8; Prov. 29:2)

Today's softness in punishment reigns from the home to the church to the state. It appears that all too frequently the offender receives greater protection than does the offended! Headlines such as "Thirty-Eight Who Saw the Murder Didn't Call the Police" have done two things: They reveal the apathy which is present among us and evoke numerous editorials, lengthy conversations and ulcer-making discussions. The older generation, observing the moral breakdown, blames the younger generation; and the younger generation, beholding the hypocrisy of the day, blames the older generation. Yet all the while there is a philosophy which is sapping the very heart of our great nation.

A. The Reason for Softness

Obviously something is happening to make such drastic changes. Simply stated it is this: *The rules of the game are undergoing change.*

God and His Word are excluded. Once God's Word controlled the decisions of our government and our courts. Punishment was meted out as the just penalty for crimes committed.

Walter Lippmann saw this change coming in his day. In his book, *The Preface to Morals* (1929), he showed that a switch from the living and true God to the created god of the liberal mind would change the moral standards and stamina of America. His conclusion is apparent today!

To teach that man is the product of evolution without responsibility to the supreme God and that there is no destiny beyond the few days of this life which is destined to annihilation, is to foster an attitude of "eat, drink and be merry, for tomorrow we die."

The result of this kind of thinking has evoked strong language on the part of editors. Bob Wiedrich of the *Chicago Tribune* wrote: "The criminal gets all the breaks. . . . Crime does pay . . . well. Ask any professional practitioner." Mr. Wiedrich

17

attributes this breakdown in justice to the tipping of the scale in favor of the accused to the place where the jailing of a criminal gives great odds to the wrongdoer. Fewer are jailed. (The sentence for murder, if you are under sixteen in one of our great states, is less than two years.)

Appealing once again to the Scriptures we find that when "the righteous are in authority, the people rejoice: but when the wicked beareth rule, the people mourn" (Prov. 29:2). The designation "wicked" in this text is used in the Old Testament of those who walk apart from God's Word and His authority! Without question the answer to our plight in regard to honest punishment for crimes committed will be realized only through a spiritual revival which enthrones God and His moral standard of right and wrong!

Prepare To Discuss Intelligently

1. How important is it to establish character in children through home training?

2. Does permissive living generate more crime and less control of the criminal?

3. What can an individual do to encourage spiritual revival in America?

4. Has the abolishing of capital punishment increased the problem of murder in America?

5. Does the philosophy of modern sociology and psychology tend toward leniency in punishment?

CHAPTER 3

The Gambling Fever

by DONALD M. BRONG, State Representative of Iowa
Association of Regular Baptist Churches

BIBLE PORTIONS TO READ: Exodus 20:1-17;
Philippians 2:1-30

TREMENDOUS and even terrible changes are
taking place over the entire world. Those looking for a better place produced by man's efforts are
either discouraged or have had to extend their
prophesied Utopia dateline. Among the ills coming
to the United States is the gambling fever. Practiced extensively in most other parts of the world
at one time or another, this strange disease is
gradually becoming part of the American way of
life and a nightmare in the American dream.

The February 1975 issue of *Reader's Digest* in a
condensed article from *The New York Times* by
Steve Cady spoke of the "compulsive gambler."
He stated:

> There are perhaps 6,000,000 compulsive
> gamblers in the United States. All of them, ac-
> cording to an increasing number of psychiatrists
> and medical authorities, are sick—walking

plagues, often causing suffering to a dozen others whose lives they touch. The compulsion ruins careers, breaks up families and leads its victims into moral deterioration, misery, bankruptcy, prison, even suicide.

Written from the standpoint of pure secularism, it reveals the alarm with which the author views the new United States gambling fever. Quickly we concede that 6 million addicts, although many, does not compare with the vastly greater number of alcoholics or habitual drug users; but as a somewhat new mania, it is a startling figure and rising rapidly.

I. What Is Gambling?

A. A Definition

Lycurgus M. Starkey, Jr., has stated in *Money Mania and Morals:*

> Legal accuracy would distinguish three requirements for any activity to be defined as gambling. First, there must be a prize or payoff in money or merchandise. Secondly, the awarding of this prize must be largely by chance, though skill may be involved in some games. In the third place, eligibility for the prize must depend not only upon the chance to win, but on a necessary payment of consideration in either money or merchandise by the player.

The above author lists forms of gambling as: (1) Betting on horse and dog racing; (2) betting on sports events; (3) lotteries, sweepstakes and bingo; (4) policy or numbers games; (5) dice and card games; (6) slot machines and "pay-off" pinball machines. Another area that might be called pseudo-gambling would include the many radio and TV game shows. It would appear that gambling is an attempt to get something for nothing, something at someone else's expense. Commencing with the innocent marble game of junior boys to playing the big games of Las Vegas, it is gambling.

B. Some Things Gambling Is Not

Some things must be listed as not falling into the category of this evil. Life is not a gamble. Farming, rearing a family, honest investments, insurance, etc., cannot be classed as gambling. The child of God is to "walk by faith, not by sight" (2 Cor. 5:7). Compare Romans 8:28; Philippians 4:11, 12 and Hebrews 11:6.

Casting of "lots" in the Bible cannot be considered gambling. The Hebrew *gōräl* means a pebble and *chebel* means a measuring line or portion. The Greek *lagchanō* means to cast lots as in Luke 1:9 and *klēros* means pebble or bit of wood with which to cast lots as in Acts 1:26. Dr. Merrill Unger states in his Bible Dictionary: "Among the Jews . . . the use of lots, with a religious intention, direct or indirect, prevailed extensively. The religious estimate . . . may be gathered from Proverbs 16:33." Historical or ritual instances listed in the above named dictionary are: (1) Choice of men for an invading force (Judg. 1:1-3); (2) partition of Palestine among the tribes (Num. 26:55; Josh. 18:10; Acts 13:19), of Jerusalem, i.e., probably its spoil or captives among captors (Obad. 11) (compare Joel 3:3; Nahum 3:10 and Matthew 27:35); (3) settlement of doubtful questions (Prov. 16:33; 18:18), a mode of divination among the heathen by means of arrows—two inscribed and one without

21

A Verse To Memorize

"And whatsoever ye do in word or deed, do all in the name of the Lord Jesus, giving thanks to God and the Father by him" (Col. 3:17).

mark (Ezek. 21:21), detection of a criminal (Josh. 7:14, 18), appointment of persons to offices or duties, as the priests (Luke 1:9), successor to Judas (Acts 1:26) and selection of a scapegoat on the Day of Atonement (Lev. 16:8, 10).

Let no one think of congregational voting in the local church for selection of persons or deciding of issues as gambling.

C. An Expensive Recreation

Gambling is a most expensive form of recreation. Horace Daggett of the Iowa Legislature calls gambling "the rich man's recreation and the poor man's disaster." Reports indicate in one state where pari-mutuel betting is legalized, out of every four persons playing the horses, one wins, two break even and one loses more than the winner won. Again we quote Mr. Starkey:

> The odds are stacked against the player in the various professionally operated gambling enterprises. The margin the professional has against you ranges from 15 to 60 percent. This is true even at the legal race tracks of the country. The track and the government between them take as much as 15 to 22 percent out of the pot before winnings are divided. If you want to make money in horse racing, don't gamble; own a track.
>
> It is common knowledge in gambling circles

that big gamblers die poor. The professional doesn't gamble. He takes an assured profit out of the money you want to lose. In the numbers or policy game, a winner should take home 1,000 to one, but the operators usually pay only 600 to 1 and often deducting 10 percent of the winnings ... thus of 1,000 bettors who pay one dollar each, or a total of $1,000, only one will win, on the average, $540.

"Mathematicians have shown that the chances of loss become greater and greater as the gambler continues to play and the resources of the house increase compared to those of the gambler," states statistician Ernest Blanche, student of gambling for twenty-five years in his book entitled *You Can't Win*.

Payoff of individuals to big business gambling has been reported as high as a possible $50 billion in 1964. This was more than was spent for private education and research, more than spent for welfare and religious activities, more than the combined profits of the 100 largest U.S. manufacturing corporations (a little in excess of $8 billion annually) of the same period.

Steve Cady acknowledges our national lust for gambling by saying, "In modern America, where government-encouraged betting has become as respectable as apple pie, an estimated 50 million citizens gamble regularly about $100 billion a year." If these figures are correct, the gambling fever has doubled in 12 years.

The cost to the nation is astronomical. Some have argued the state revenue received is worth the problems. It is a proven fact that crime and security cost goes up when betting comes in. In one state with legalized pari-mutuel betting facts

23

show that out of 859 employees at the track, 205 are for security purposes. The claim that parimutuel betting will benefit the state is wrong. It will cost the state more than it will bring in revenue. It is estimated that one state is promised $4 million in taxes after a 3—5 year period if they will but legalize gambling. The state operating budget (1975-76) totals more than $1,120,000,000 or about ¼ of 1 percent. People are being shown the $4 million as if the state could hardly exist without it. We dare to say it will cost the state more than the expected revenue in enlarged security forces, loss of employment, loss of time, loss of homes and loss of life.

Again Lycurgus M. Starkey has written:

> Reno, Nevada, has the highest crime rate of any city in the U.S. in proportion to its population. Its suicides are twice the American average. It ranks in murders with cities four times its size. Four times as many policemen are needed than the American average for a comparable population. Welfare and other costs are abnormal.

President Harry Truman said, "If you want to be like Nevada, that's your business. Nevada is the only black spot on the U.S. continent. . . . Legalized gambling is the worst thing in the world. I don't believe in it. Too many people have jumped out of windows because of Nevada. It is a fever." Most assuredly such a statement was made without any thought to Biblical standard as the entire quote could not be printed. However, it is to be observed that the former President's attitude regarding the benefits of gambling to the state was definite opposition. If he was correct regarding Nevada, then consider the condition of our nation now and the part gambling must be playing in the rapidly rising crime rate.

II. Gambling Is Sin

A. Poor Management of Money

It has been shown that the risk of returns is very great and becomes a foolish waste of money. Christians should consider everything they possess as belonging to God: "Glorify God in your body, and in your spirit, which are God's" (1 Cor. 6:20). They will want to be faithful to the trust (1 Cor. 4:2). Compare Matthew 25:14-30. There is a day coming when we must give account of what we did with what was given us (2 Cor. 5:9, 10). We are to be "not slothful in business; fervent in spirit; serving the Lord" (Rom. 12:11).

Christian people should be constantly conscious that everything they do must please Him Who loved us and gave Himself for our redemption (Col. 3:17).

B. Harmful to Others

Terrible facts may be multiplied how people have injured friends and family just for the thrill of trying for wealth without working.

Our Bible teaches that we are our brother's keeper (Phil. 2:3, 4). We will not steal from the world, let alone from our brothers in Christ (Exod. 20:15; Rom. 2:21; Eph. 4:28). Gambling is a form of stealing.

C. Habit-Forming

The headline in the aforementioned *Reader's Digest* article is a too true statement. "Doctors are beginning to rate gambling as a disease on par with alcoholism and drug addiction. It may be our most widespread unrecognized illness."

Dr. Robert L. Custer, chief of staff at the Brecksville, Ohio, Veteran Hospital feels strongly that "compulsive gambling is a psychological addiction . . . classified as a disease." His patients experience withdrawal syndromes of two-weeks' duration accompanied with "reaction ranging from restlessness to shakiness, severe headaches and diarrhea."

Gambling Anonymous, started in 1957, now has 5,000 members in 250 chapters. Like Alcoholics Anonymous, its therapeutic value is by long sessions of confession, discussion of common problems and efforts to assist one another by phone checkups, etc., because "they live only one bet from disaster." Dr. Custer states, "It's the same as an alcoholic taking that first drink." Testimony given at a G.A. session, as related by the *Digest* article, revealed the power of such a habit on a seventeen-year-old youth. He told the group he had slashed his hand with a knife. "I told my parents the loan sharks did it, and I needed $300. I took the money to the track and lost it all."

We confess it is difficult to understand the parents, loan sharks and track operators. With such a combination we understand the youth.

Some 6,000,000 people in the United States are classified as "compulsive gamblers." Many others are near the breaking point with the number increasing. No Christian should be numbered in such a captivated and sickly multitude. Christ died to set us free from the bondage of this world (Rom. 8:15; Gal. 5:1). Christians are free people (John

8:32, 36; Rom. 6:18, 22; 2 Tim. 2:4).

D. Roots in Covetousness

Covetousness is to greedily desire something that belongs to someone else. A fundamental law from the heart of God is "thou shalt not covet" (Exod. 20:17). Our all-wise Father knew the ills that would come from this satanic greed. The word "covet" in different forms occurs some forty times in the Bible. We note the importance of despising this sin and its destructive results (Luke 12:15; Eph. 5:3; Col. 3:5; Heb. 13:5; 2 Pet. 2:3).

III. Gambling Can Be Overcome

A. National Level

Nationally and governmentally it will require an informed citizenry demanding legislation to remove this blight from our society. History reveals the sad fact that this is accomplished only after sufficient numbers become alarmed at the destructiveness in homes, fortunes and lives. Informing elected lawmakers of our concern for our nation and displeasure with legalized gambling is effective. Being informed so that we may speak and write intelligently will be helpful.

B. Individual Level

Individually it must be treated as any sin Christ died to remove. The cure is the Christ of the cross (John 1:29; Heb. 4:14-16; 9:28; 1 John 1:9; 2:1, 2).

Conclusion

No Christian should be found contributing to the

wealth of racketeers, sharks and other undesirables that make merchandise of the participants. No Christian need be bound by anything designed by the father of liars, Satan.

Christians are free people and should consider themselves and all they possess to belong to God.

Prepare To Discuss Intelligently

1. What is gambling?

2. Why is it possible that some people become gambling addicts?

3. Is gambling sin? Why?

4. What can be done to rid gambling from our nation?

5. Is there any habit contrary to God's will which is too difficult for a Christian to overcome (Rev. 3:21; 21:7)?

CHAPTER 4

Our Social Responsibilities

by ERNEST PICKERING, TH.D., President of Baptist
  Bible College of Pennsylvania and Baptist Bible
  School of Theology

BIBLE PORTIONS TO READ: James 2:1-4, 14-20;
Acts 9:36-43; 11:27-30; Romans 13:1-14; James
5:1-9

OUR AGE is filled with social problems and
  those seeking solutions to them. The public
media is daily saturated with reports on various
kinds of social problems. Many billions of dollars
are being expended at various levels of government attempting to alleviate them. Private social agencies are spending additional millions in the
same battle.

The question is being asked with increasing
urgency, "What involvement should Christians
and their churches have in social action?" In the
last ten or fifteen years a considerable number of
books and articles on this subject have come from
the pens of evangelical writers. The major thrust of
most of these writings is to the effect that fundamental Christians have neglected their duty in the

area of social action and should become more involved. Let us examine this thesis.

I. Definitions

What do we mean by "social responsibilities"? Webster's Dictionary declares that the word *social* means "having to do with human beings living together as a group in a situation requiring that they have dealings with one another." The word encompasses a broad spectrum of human relationships in the home, business, school, government and elsewhere.

Responsibilities are our obligations toward others which relate, in this context, to the alleviation of their suffering, deprivation or physical and material needs.

II. Distinctions

A. Between Israel and America

Evangelical writers who are pleading for more Christian involvement in social reform programs tend to rest heavily on Old Testament passages to defend their appeals. They cite passages from Old Testament prophets who condemned national unrighteousness and called the nation to repentance. They pointed out that the prophets condemned materialism (Isa. 1:22, 23), unfair use of labor (Jer. 22:13; Mal. 3:5), oppression of the poor (Amos 5:11), perversion of justice (Hab. 1:2-4) and other such human evils. The prophets, say some modern evangelicals, were seeking to "clean up" their society. We should do the same if we claim to love righteousness.

There is a fundamental difference, however, between ancient Israel and modern America. Israel was a theocracy, a religious-political state governed by Jehovah God. She had a national religion, and God gave her political structure. No other nation on earth has ever had such a relationship to God, and none ever will. Israel was chosen to be a "special people . . . above all people that are upon the face of the earth" (Deut. 7:6).

B. Between Old Testament Prophets and New Testament Preachers

Today's call from some quarters is for men who will live the "prophetic" voice. This means a crusading attack on all sorts of social ills and a concerted, organized effort to remove them. Senator Mark Hatfield of Oregon has been a noted leader in promoting this line of thought. Speaking as an evangelical Christian and politician Hatfield wrote: "Our prophets are those concerned chiefly with seeing God's purposes for the world being realized. They hear a call for the 'kingdom of God' to be furthered on earth, and are concerned about the problems of war, poverty, and social injustice. Following in the tradition of the Old Testament prophets, they are not afraid to judge the

31

social and political establishment" ("The Total Minister," *Eternity,* September, 1975).

Unfortunately such appeals are not grounded on sound theology and a proper understanding of God's Word. God's purposes for this age do not include an organized, religious campaign against social injustice. This ministry will be undertaken by the Lord Himself in a future millennial age. Then there will be universal peace, a stable economy and other social benefits now impossible to attain (cf. Mic. 4:1-5). Hatfield's call for "pastor-prophets" is a misguided one, for there is no such spiritual gift being bestowed on the church today. The very title given to the shepherd of the flock—pastor-teacher—excludes any thought that he is a "prophet" (cf. Eph. 4:11, 12). The man of God today is to expound the Scriptures and to build up the saints "for the work of the ministry," thus causing the Body of Christ to grow. The primary business of the preacher in this Church Age is not to "speak to the conscience of the nation" (a phrase popular in these days), but to teach the spiritual truths of God's Word for the purposes of winning the lost to Christ and establishing believers in the faith. The Old Testament prophets were religious spokesmen to a nation because they were divinely appointed to a theocracy, a political society, an organized nation governed by God. Neither America nor any other nation is such a society nor has such a prophetic ministry.

Strictly speaking, there is no appeal to national repentance in the time in which we live. We find no invitation in the New Testament for Gentile nations to repent and turn to God. The appeal to the gospel of Christ is *individual,* not *national.* While respecting the concern and sincerity of those who apply the promise of 2 Chronicles 7:14 to modern America, it was never so directed. It was to a specific, covenant nation and a valid promise only to them within the Old Testament context.

C. Between the Organized Church and the Individual Believer

Examples of great Christians of the past are sometimes given in order to prod believers on to a greater social involvement. One of the most frequently cited is William Wilberforce, an English Christian of considerable influence in his day (1759-1833). He was a great opponent of the slave trade and is hailed as a monumental example of Christian social concern in action.

Remember, however, that Wilberforce acted within the context of his own situation. He was a political leader, a member of the British parliament for many years. He conducted his social efforts within this context. We don't say that he never sought to enlist assistance from fellow-believers, but we note that his responsibilities lay within the realm of government; and he sought social reform in that realm. As an individual Christian acting within his sphere of duty as a government leader, he opposed the slave trade. Not every believer has the same responsibility Wilberforce had, however; nor do local churches have such an obligation. There is a distinction to be made between an individual believer's responsibility as a private citizen of a nation or as an elected official thereof, and his duty as a functioning member of an organized church.

III. Declaration

A. Believers Should Be Characterized by Compassion for Men in Their Needs

It is certainly true that too often Christians are like the priest and the Levite who, beholding the wounded Jew on the road, "passed by on the other side" (Luke 10:30-32). While we must ever maintain a proper theological view of the Church's ministry here on earth, we must not forget that our Lord wept at the sight of human suffering (John 11:35). It is all too possible for us, fed and clothed as we are, to become smug and complacent and fail to be moved at the sight of staggering human needs.

B. The Church Has Not Been Commissioned To Remedy Social Ills

"Absolutely no evidence exists that the apostolic church projected even one solution for the most pressing world problems of its day. . . . The import of the Biblical evidence is that whatever was accomplished was not realized through a social program or a social impact, but rather by the power of God the Holy Spirit as the message of the gospel was preached to individuals" (John Witmer, "Christian Social Responsibility," *Bibliotheca Sacra*, July, 1953, p. 217). Even Walter Rauschenbusch who is called the "father of the social gospel" declared, "It is correctly asserted that the apostles undertook no social propaganda" (*Christianity and the Social Crisis*, p. 152).

Study the last words of the Lord before He ascended into Heaven (Matt. 28:18-20). There is nothing here even remotely to suggest a social program to remedy societal ills. It is a spiritual program to bring men to saving faith in Christ and to assist them in growing in His grace. Luke's account concurs with Matthew's emphasis (Luke 24:44-48).

C. Human Society Will Deteriorate Continually and Is Doomed to Judgment

Those who favor more evangelical efforts to change the course of human society for the better generally are critical of this view. One outstanding spokesman of an evangelical social action program lays the blame for evangelical failure in this area to the fact that large numbers of Christians hold to a dispensational interpretation of the Bible (as found in the Scofield Reference Bible) which emphasized "man's continuing inability either to do good or to please God" (Richard Quebedeaux, *The Young Evangelicals,* p. 80). This is perceptive and, we believe, correct (though without acknowledging "blame"). However, the answer to the problem is not to repudiate dispensationalism as Quebedeaux and others have done, but rather to accept what God's Word teaches and act thereupon. Scripture certainly teaches a progressive deterioration religiously, morally and politically as Christ's coming draws near (cf. 2 Tim. 4:1-4; 1 Tim. 4:1-3; 2 Thess. 2:1 ff.). Hopes for the betterment of society as a whole cannot be based on any teaching of Scripture since passages supporting this hope do not exist.

The objection to the pessimistic view of human civilization is felt by those who have hopes and are extending efforts to lift man's society to a higher plane by social means. Those who predict failure upon the basis of an exegesis of Scripture are labeled as promoters of gloom and often are represented as heartless. They are simply seeking to be Biblical.

D. The Individual Believer Does Have Social Responsibilities

Within the compass of this lesson it would be impossible to discuss all the social responsibilities of the believer. However, some examples will suffice.

For instance, believers are to obey the laws of the land and seek to live in proper relationship with their government. "Let every soul be subject unto the higher powers" (Rom. 13:1). Government officials are declared to be "God's ministers" (Rom. 13:4, 6). Where laws of the land come into direct conflict with doctrines of Scripture, the believer must "obey God rather than men" (Acts 5:29). However, this refers to matters of definite doctrinal or ethical conflicts and not merely to personal desires, wishes or dreams.

Certainly domestic obligations face believers. The husband is to love and care for his wife; the wife is to respect and help her husband; and the children should obey their parents (Eph. 5:22—6:2). There are many instructions concerning the Christian home in the New Testament.

Christians are to maintain a good testimony toward their employers (Col. 3:22, 23). Likewise Christian employers are responsible to pay their workers a living wage (Col. 4:1). Labor is viewed as honorable and beneficial, and concepts of a "welfare state" find no support in Scripture (2 Thess. 3:6-10).

There is a place for just "doing good" (Heb. 13:16). Obviously this ought not to be stretched to involve senseless and harmful programs which waste money and hinder the development of self-reliance in individuals. However, Christians ought to stand ready to help their neighbor, whoever he is and whatever his spiritual state.

Often this kind of good works can open the way to give a testimony of God's saving grace. On this basis some believers become involved in Red Cross work, in local community projects, in service in a hospital or other institution offering aid to the needy. There is a distinction to be made between individual, personalized good works and an attempt—through organized religious power structures—to revolutionize society as a whole. Paul was especially concerned that believers maintain good works before others; and in his epistle to Titus he mentioned this subject several times (Titus 1:16; 2:7, 14; 3:1, 2, 8, 14). We are not saved *by* good works (Titus 3:5), but we are certainly saved *for* good works (Eph. 2:10).

It should be noted that the *emphasis of the New Testament is on the believer's responsibilities to assist his fellow believers in their physical and material needs*. Study these Scriptures: Galatians 2:10; Romans 15:24, 25 and 1 Timothy 5:16. This is not to say that the believer has no responsibility to help alleviate human suffering in general. He does have a *primary* responsibility toward fellow Christians. This fact is often overlooked by writers and speakers who quote New Testament passages exhorting believers toward social action as though those passages were urging them to support government social programs, enlist in the Peace Corps or carry banners in some sort of demonstration against poverty or unemployment.

The correct balance given by the Apostle Paul is found in Galatians 6:10. While we have a responsibility toward men in general, our primary one is to believers.

F. The Local Church Has Social Responsibilities

Congregations of believers were exhorted by the Apostles to provide care for those who needed care among them. There were many widows among the early churches, and those were to be supported (1 Tim. 5:3-16). Believers who were poor or in need were to be succored by the churches (Acts 11:29; 20:35; Rom. 12:13; 1 Tim. 6:18; Heb. 13:16). By these admonitions God certainly seems to declare the principle of private responsibility for those in need and especially enforces upon His people the necessity of proper care for fellow Christians.

In order to fulfill their obligations many believers and churches choose to support Christian agencies such as those approved by the GARBC. In these agencies they have born-again, well-trained and experienced persons who are ministering to the needs of homeless children, retarded children, the elderly, widows and others.

Prepare To Discuss Intelligently

1. Should a Christian give to the United Fund?

2. What social concern does your church manifest? Through what channels?

3. Do you think it is in accord with Biblical principles to redistribute America's wealth, taking from the more affluent to give to the poor?

CHAPTER 5

Role of Women in the Church

by PAUL TASSELL, PH.D., Pastor of Grandview Park
  Baptist Church, Des Moines, IA

BIBLE PORTIONS TO READ: Proverbs 31:10-31;
1 Corinthians 11:8-12; 1 Timothy 2:9-15; 1 Peter
3:1-8

IN THIS STUDY we are not concerned with
  what Ms. Lucy Liberation thinks. Nor are we
seeking to understand the philosophy of Ms.
Frieda Feminist. Our purpose is to learn what
God's Word, the Bible, has to say about the proper
role of womanhood.

Our study, therefore, accepts three general but
important assumptions. First, *woman, like man, is
the direct creation of God*. We categorically reject
the hypothesis of evolution with all of its implications. Second, *the Bible is the inspired, inerrant,
infallible Word of God*. What the Bible teaches
about womanhood is God's revelation about her
valid role. Third, *a Spirit-led woman will desire to
be obedient to the Word of God*. God's authority
must take priority over popular feminist fads and
fancies. These basic assumptions prepare us for
our study.

I. Her Magnificent Person

Heathen, pagan societies—both ancient and modern—have failed to recognize woman's proper role. She was demeaned to the common level of slavery by the ancient pagans. Legally and socially she was under the complete domination of her husband. She was exploited for the purpose of childbearing; and when those reproductive functions were passé, her remaining years were spent as a virtual slave. Modern pagan cultures treat their women similarly.

The God of the Bible did not, however, present Adam with a slave. The account of woman's creation is found in Genesis 2:20-25. She was referred to as "an help meet for him" (v. 20). She was taken from Adam's side (v. 21). She constituted a distinctive creation from the hand of God (v. 22). Adam defined her magnificent personhood in the words of 2:23. Eve was not property; she was a person. She was not minor or menial but magnificent and meaningful to Adam.

Paul masterfully expressed the distinctive difference between the sexes in 1 Corinthians 11:1-15. Unisex is not the will of God. Man is to be masculine. Woman is to be feminine. A woman should act like a woman, speak like a woman, dress like a woman and be content to be the feminine person God intended her to be.

II. Her Marital Principles

Eve was the first bride and no doubt a very beautiful one. She was the world's first wife. Read our Savior's words in Matthew 19:4-6. Marriage began with God. The marital relationship was established by an all-wise Heavenly Father for the happiness and wholeness of both man and woman.

Since God is the Author of marriage, we are wise to look to Him for marital principles. The Bible reveals some specific and simple, yet profound, principles which should guide every Christian woman maritally. First, marriage is a *sacred* relationship. Read Romans 7:2. Paul's statement is in keeping with the Seventh Commandment, "Thou shalt not commit adultery" (Exod. 20:14). Easy divorce laws notwithstanding, God's law commands a lifelong sanctifying (setting apart) of a wife to her husband. God intends for marriage to be a sacred, lasting union.

Second, marriage is, for woman, a *submissive* relationship. Peter exhorted wives to be "in subjection unto their own husbands: even as Sara obeyed Abraham, calling him lord" (1 Pet. 3:5, 6). This is not the word of a male chauvinist. Peter wrote under the inspiration of the Holy Spirit for our blessing and profit. In fact, the context of Peter's exhortation has to do with saved wives winning unsaved husbands to the Lord. The principle of wifely submission is the key to such soul-winning success.

Third, marriage is a *spiritual* relationship. This *principle* is expressed as a *picture* by Paul in Ephesians 5:22-33. The wife pictures the earthly Bride of Christ, the Church. The husband symbolizes the heavenly Bridegroom, Jesus Christ. The spiritual relationship is the very heart of a beautiful marriage. That is why Paul emphasizes that a Christian woman marry "only in the Lord" (1 Cor. 7:39). Moreover, Paul's warning against the "unequal yoke" is based on the importance of the spiritual nature of this highest of all human relationships. A

Christian woman's submission to her husband is, therefore, placed on the highest plateau when she realizes that submission to be akin to the submissive relationship of the Church to the Headship of Christ.

Fourth, marriage is a *sexual* relationship. A "mania for manuals," sex manuals, has seemingly gripped our adult population. Sadly, even some nominally Christian publishing houses have printed inane and superficial (even silly) books on how wives can entice their own husbands! The Holy Spirit, however, simply and soberly counsels us in the words of 1 Corinthians 7:4 and 5. Read carefully. The sexual aspect of marriage will only be what God intended for the woman when it includes the sacred, submissive and spiritual characteristics.

III. Her Maternal Prerogatives

Breathes there a woman with soul so dead whose ears have never heard the words, "I'm just a housewife"? Is it really true that the hand that rocks the cradle rules the world? Is motherhood a second-class calling? In answer we should look carefully at the words of one of the most beautiful and instructive passages in the Bible, Proverbs

42

31:10-31. Psalms 127 and 128 are also God's Word concerning maternal prerogatives and privileges. Peter spoke of husbands and wives as being "heirs together of the grace of life" (1 Pet. 3:7).

We must note that it is a woman's privileged prerogative *to be a homemaker*. Our divorce-demented, abortion-aberrant society has systematically and shamefully rebelled against God's role for spouses in Genesis 1:28. The Bible speaks of motherhood as majestic and homemaking as honorable.

It is also a woman's privileged prerogative to *guide the home*. Read the inspired words of 1 Timothy 5:14. A husband ought to carefully, fairly and prayerfully give his wife sufficent cash to run the household and adequate affection to show his appreciation for her expertise.

Ephesians 5:22—6:4 teaches that important privilege and prerogative of *loving submission to the husband*. If her children are to learn respect for and admiration of the father, the wife must teach by her example of such respect and admiration. It is the prerogative of a wife to make a home a haven and a foretaste of Heaven. On the other hand, she can choose to make her husband miserable and her children cantankerous by her self-will. Twice in the Book of Proverbs we are warned: "It is better to dwell in a corner of the housetop, than with a brawling woman in a wide house" (Prov. 21:9; 25:24).

Perhaps the primary prerogative of a mother is the privilege of *molding the pliable minds and hearts of her children to the blessed will and Word of God*. How blessed is the world because of soul-winning mothers! How fortunate is the child

43

whose mother teaches him discipline, duty and devotion! A mother who invests her life in those of her children will be richly "blessed; her husband also, and he praiseth her" (Prov. 31:28).

IV. Her Ecclesiastical Privileges

Dr. Luke has given us some very significant information about the crowd which met in the upper room and would become the first church (Acts 1:14). That early group of disciples included women! No honest reading of the early history of the New Testament church can overlook the importance of women in that church.

Involved in ecclesiastical responsibilities for women are both prohibitions and privileges. A woman is not to have authority over men in a church. Paul made this very clear in 1 Timothy 2:11-15. This first pastoral epistle also prohibits women from holding the offices of pastor and deacon. A bishop or pastor is to be "the husband of one wife"; he is to be "a man" (in verses 1, 2 and 5 of 1 Timothy 3). Likewise, the deacons are to be "the husbands of one wife" (1 Tim. 3:12). The ordaining of women pastors is patently unscriptural.

Happily, there are many privileges to be enjoyed as a woman in a local church. When Paul ministered in Thessalonica, his message was met with accepting response from many "and of the chief women not a few" (Acts 17:4). Later Paul and Silas went to Berea where "many of them believed; also of honourable women which were Greeks, and of men, not a few" (Acts 17:12). No doubt Paul had women such as these in mind when he wrote "that women adorn themselves in modest apparel" (1 Tim. 2:9). What a privilege for a Christian woman to honor Christ by testifying of her faith even by her fashions. Paul also spoke of women adorning themselves "with good works" (1 Tim. 2:10). In Titus 2:3-5 Paul gave further instruction regarding the role of women in the local church. Although women are forbidden to teach men, women "may teach the young women . . . that the word of God be not blasphemed" (Titus 2:4, 5).

Women may serve the Lord in the areas of prayer, music, teaching, typing and visitation with great profit to the church and great satisfaction to the feminine heart.

V. Her Societal Professions

Most of what we have written thus far applies primarily to married homemakers. What about the single lady and the widow? What are their roles? Surely God calls some women into professions other than homemaking! Examples of New Testament women who were obviously "career women" can be cited: Dorcas (Acts 9:36), Lydia (Acts 16:14) and some of the women listed by Paul in Romans 16.

The role of women in society is much debated today, but two guidelines ought to be part and parcel of the godly woman's professional philosophy. First, whatever I do must enhance and not debilitate the homelife of America. My children must not take second place to a career. My life's work must strengthen the Christian home.

Second, whatever I do must be in keeping with Biblical principles of life. Christian society in particular and the world in general have profited greatly from women missionaries, nurses, teachers, secretaries, editors, writers, musicians, administrators, etc. Women are entering the fields of politics, business and industry in unprecedented numbers. Christian women must be sensitive to the two guidelines mentioned above as they seek God's perfect will.

VI. Her Scriptural Prototypes

Women are prominent in Scripture. From Eve to Esther, from Deborah to Dorcas, from Miriam to Mary are a host of women whose lives serve as prototypes or models after which twentieth-century women may pattern their principles and practices. As a magnificent creation of God, Eve is to be studied closely. Her tragic deception by Satan prompted Paul to cite Eve as an illustration of susceptibility to Satan's guile (2 Cor. 11:3). Paul also wrote: "And Adam was not deceived, but the woman being deceived was in the transgression" (1 Tim. 2:14). We see, therefore, the value of studying the lives of Old Testament women in order to discern what may be the *peculiar weaknesses* of womanhood.

Analyzing Scriptural women also is helpful in ascertaining *positive strengths* of womanhood. Peter called attention to Sara (1 Pet. 3) as an example of a winsome wife with proper marital principles. Hannah and Jochebed were examples of maternal prerogatives. In the New Testament, Paul praised Lois and Eunice for their maternal ministries (2 Tim. 1:5). Mary, the mother of Jesus, and Elizabeth, the mother of John the Baptist, ought to be carefully and prayerfully studied by every Christian woman. Priscilla and Phoebe

46

are examples of ecclesiastical excellence as they devoted themselves to New Testament church activity. Deborah, Esther and Lydia were career women whose personalities were individualistic but instructive. The Holy Spirit doubtless included so much female biography in Holy Writ for the very reason that God is concerned that women know what their role in life is to be.

Prepare To Discuss Intelligently

1. Why is unisex contrary to Biblical, sexual identification?

2. How may Biblical marital principles be practically worked out in everyday home life?

3. Why are mothers the key to citizens who respect and obey authority?

4. Where do women play the most vital part in the work and ministry of a local church?

5. How may a professional woman effectively advance the cause of Christ?

6. Why is it necessary and profitable to study the lives of Biblical women?

CHAPTER 6

The Christian and the Jew

by ELMER UBBINK, Missionary to the Jewish
   Peoples, with Baptist Mid-Missions, Los Angeles
   Hebrew Mission

BIBLE PORTIONS TO READ: Genesis 12:1-8;
Isaiah 62:6, 7; Jeremiah 31:31-37; Ezekiel 3:17-
19; 34:1-10; Romans 9:1—11:36

L ORD BEACONSFIELD said: "The attempt
   to extirpate the Jew has been made under the
most favorable auspices, on the largest scale, and
for the longest period of time. Egyptian Pharaohs,
Assyrian kings, Roman emperors, Scandinavian
crusaders, Gothic princes, and holy inquisitors
have alike devoted their energies to the fulfillment
of this common purpose. Expatriation, exile, cap-
tivity, confiscation, torture, and massacre on the
most extensive and ingenious scale have been tried
in vain. The Jew, however, remains!"

We of the twentieth century have tried to form
opinions and forge political solutions to an age-old
problem which dates back to Satan's rebellion
against God and his antagonism toward the Redeemer and redemption.

Israel as a nation occupies a peculiar place in God's economy. The miracles recorded in the Bible which rehearse God's providence toward this people become a train of evidences which demonstrate God's sovereign choice of a man, his family and the nation from his loins. God made His choice so He could fulfill His promise of a Redeemer for Adam's sons.

Ford Ottman wrote by way of illustration: "The ability of the whale to swallow Jonah is no more wonderful than its inability to assimilate him. If God be not reckoned with, neither the one nor the other can be explained."[1] Neither can Israel nor her preservation be explained without reckoning with God and His covenant promises.

We will discuss three areas in this lesson: Our attitude toward the Jewish person, toward the Jewish people or nation and toward the promises or Word of God.

I. Our Attitude Toward the Jewish Person

Perhaps we should understand at the outset that the Jew believes there is only one brand of Christian. He is the one who descended from a long line of persecutors who came in Christ's name and the sign of the cross. The average Jew believes that all Gentiles may be lumped together as Christians. Last year Meir Kahane, head of the Jewish Defense League, spoke of the fundamentalist and evangelical Christian Protestant sects as believing the words of God to Abraham, "Blessed is he that blesseth thee, and cursed is he that curseth thee"

---

[1] Ford C. Ottman, *"God's Oath,"* (New York: Our Hope Publishing Company) p. 225.

(Num. 24:9). He said that the Israeli government still clings to the myth that real Christians are dangerous to Jews whereas real Christians could be a distinct help to the preservation of the nation today. Someone else put it this way—Israel turns to her real enemies as friends and looks upon her real friends as enemies.

A. The Christian As Being 'in Christ'

Doesn't Christ's love constrain us to love the lost? If the Jew without Christ is lost, then you and I as believers "in Christ" have a constraint and burden upon us to reach that Jewish person with the message of grace in Christ. The logic is as simple as this: If I am a Christian, then I must manifest the Spirit of Christ, His compassion.

The heart of God is bared before us as we listen to the words of the Lord Jesus from His house of prayer, the Temple in Jerusalem, as recorded in Matthew 23:37-39. Again we feel the wet of the tears of God as we read the Lord Jehovah's words in Deuteronomy 5:29. Repeatedly throughout the Old Testament the Lord pleaded with Israel to walk in His ways (e.g., Josh. 24:15; 1 Kings 18:17-39; Ps. 81:13; Isa. 1:18; 43:1-28; 45:22; 48:18; Ezek. 18:30-32), and we behold the tender compassion so manifest when He walked the paths of the Land. Finally, read His words by Jeremiah in Jeremiah 9:1. This is the compassionate love of the Lord for Israel. Dare we compare our own heart to His?

B. The Christian As a Neighbor

The Lord Jesus stated the two Great Commandments of the Law in Matthew 22:35-40. (Read them.) He quoted from Deuteronomy 6:5 and Leviticus 19:18. These commandments govern the holy walk of His holy people.

The Lord Jesus further defined what a neighbor is by the parable He told in Luke 10:30-37. The Good Samaritan was described in answer to the question, "Who is my neighbour?" and we discern that our neighbor is one to whom we are neighbor or are near. For many of you, this means that the Jewish people whose elbows you rub daily are your neighbors also. Perhaps many of you do not touch the lives of Jewish people on any day. Just remember: They are the brethren of our Lord according to the flesh. Do you not fellowship with Him daily? They are important to Him.

C. The Christian As an Evangelist

An evangelist is a bearer of good news. We tend to think of an evangelist as a professional man with a special calling, but every Christian qualifies as an evangelist or missionary. The word of reconciliation has been committed to us, and we are ambassadors for Christ for a ministry of beseeching the lost to be reconciled to God through faith in Christ. (See 2 Corinthians 5:19 and 20.)

1. *Principles of Jewish Missions.* Our particular concern is Jewish missions, and the first question queries, "How is this different?" It *is* different. There are principles to be observed. One should know something about the sufferings of this people through the centuries. Understanding what God has covenanted to this people and what He has stated concerning their future history is essential. Learning how the Old Testament reveals Christ and learning how to use the gospel verses of the

51

Old Testament with their parallels in the New Testament prove very helpful. Knowing how not to be offensive to a Jewish person but rather being winsome in the likeness of Christ will serve you in good stead as you witness to Jewish neighbors.

2. *Erroneous Interpretations.* The presence of error is often found in our thinking. Some people reason that the Jew has had it. He is not worthy of salvation, and they take their cue from Acts 13:46. (Read.) Then they skip to Acts 28:28. (Read.) These verses are used to prove that the Jew cannot have the gospel and cannot be saved. Nothing is further from the truth.

The very next book, Romans, witnesses to the fact that there is no difference between Jew and Gentile; both are sinners before God (Rom. 3:23). Although the Jew has the advantage of possessing the Scriptures, he is judged by them and is commended to the faith of Abraham (Rom. 4:3). All have not and will not believe, but God has not cast them away. He has reserved "a remnant according to the election of grace" of which Paul states that he is a living example (Rom. 11:1-5). It remains, then, for us to recognize the need the Jew has for salvation and to begin actively filling that need by the gospel message.

3. *Maturing the Jew in Christ.* When a Jewish person is born again in Christ, he must have a place of fellowship and spiritual growth. This means your local church should be opened to him. A believer who is Jewish cannot be placed in a Christian ghetto. He already has the idea that the church is a Gentile organization; but he must understand that the Church, the Body of Christ, is represented in the local church. The Jew and Gentile are one in Christ. If we keep our relationship to Christ in proper view, we will have no trouble making room for the Jewish person. He is not to be turned into a Gentile, but he is to be nurtured to maturity in Christ as a Christian who is a Jew.

4. *How To Reach the Jewish Person.* Christ's compassion and the Samaritan's neighborliness have already been pointed out as qualities needed in reaching Jewish people. However, they will be reached only by God's Word (Rom. 10:17, 14c).

When occupied with personal witnessing, preaching belongs in the pulpit, especially if one is witnessing to Jewish people. Gaining the confidence of a Jewish person is paramount. One must exercise love and compassion toward the Jew and tenderness toward Jesus Christ as Lord. The consistent life testimony of a Christian speaks with an authoritative voice which conveys Christ's reality to the unbeliever.

Nicodemus was a Jew. Observe how the Lord Jesus talked to him (John 3). He did not preach. He merely answered a question which was asked. Nicodemus already had a large measure of confidence in Him. Then look in on the walk to Emmaus (Luke 24:13-32) where the risen Lord Jesus walked silently many miles listening. He interjected a simple question which enabled Him to expound the Scriptures from Moses and the Prophets in order that they might know the suffering Messiah. We do not have the details of that conversation, but one could construct it easily with a study of the Messianic passages which give the predictions concerning His eternal Being, His incarnation and birth, His life, suffering, death, burial and resurrection. He is identified in the Old Testament.

Small things count much in witnessing to Jewish people. Friendliness and concern, as well as awareness and recognition, are a ministry of little things. Receiving the Jew for who he is and what he has achieved is being gracious. Promoting the natural pride in his family will win his friendship. Noting his holidays and rituals and not interfering with his Sabbath will gain his confidence. A trusted Gentile friend will be allowed to help in the family affairs and will bring an invitation to Bar Mitzvahs and weddings.

The Jew is the way he is because he has been taught by a system which will not recognize Jesus as the Messiah. Rabbinical Judaism is full of hang-ups. We can go right down the doctrines of Christ to list those hang-ups: The deity of Christ; His virgin birth; His sinless humanity, His vicarious atonement; His death, burial, resurrection and High Priestly session in Heaven. Since the Temple was destroyed in A.D. 70 and there has been no altar for the blood offering, Judaism has taught that God will accept prayer, repentance, charity and the loss of flesh and blood through fasting as an atonement for sin. This is a false hope in the works of righteousness which one does. Isaiah 9:16 states, "For the leaders of this people cause them to err; and they that are led of them are destroyed."

Let us emphasize this fact. Knowing about the Jew does not do away with the need for knowing the Scriptures. It amplifies the need for being able to give Bible answers to Jewish problems and questions. The Jewish Department of Baptist Mid-Missions publishes the *SHOFAR Magazine* quarterly in order to get such information into the hands of our pastors and people.

II. Our Attitude Toward the Jewish People

There is a need to think clearly and Biblically where the Jew and the nation of Israel are concerned. The individual Jew can and must be saved, but nationally he is under a partial blindness until the times of the Gentile nations are fulfilled.

A. Pro-Israel?

Being pro-Israel does not mean that one is necessarily anti-Arab. Both are Semites, and the gospel is meant for both. In Isaiah 19 the Lord speaks of "that day" in which both Assyria and Egypt will be included with Israel under the blessing of God. Obviously this is the time of Messiah's reign. Today Israel has not recognized her Messiah, although one day she will. That will be the day when "all Israel shall be saved" (Rom. 11:26).

Since 1948 the Nation has been restored to the land in a partial regathering at their own expense. It is thoroughly Biblical to recognize that the title deed to the Land belongs to Israel. In that day of national salvation Israel will be completely re-gathered at the Lord's expense.

B. Anti-Semitism

The definition of anti-Semitism is difficult. The dictionary states that it is opposition to Semites, especially the Jew. Anti-Semitism stems from hatred and from jealousy; but it has its roots in the satanic design against the people and the line of the Redeemer.

Zionism and the establishing of the nation have created political hatred. In the past the Jew has suffered as a religious, civil and social outcast so that hatred comes from all angles. However, the fact of God's providential care for Israel, according to His covenants, has provoked more hatred than any one cause. Reread the promise in Deuteronomy 8:18.

Check yourself. Is there a taint of hatred or jealousy in your heart? Take heed to the warning in Zechariah 2:8. He was speaking of Israel.

C. Aid to Israel

This thought may well be controversial, but planting trees (by contribution) and aiding nominally in the fund drive for Israel may afford an opportunity to witness concerning your faith that God is keeping His covenants. Your respect for the Jewish people will show.

III. Our Attitude Toward the Word of God

A. The Covenants

God stated His covenant with Abraham many times, and each time He amplified the sevenfold provisions of that covenant first made in Genesis 12:1-3. (See the old Scofield Reference Bible notes on pages 24 and 25 for a full exposition of the seven provisions of the covenant.) The additional passages are: Genesis 13:14-18; 15:1-21; 17:1-14; 22:15-18; 26:1-5; 28:13-15 and 35:10-12. The promises in this covenant certainly settle the claim of the right to the Land.

B. The Restorations

The Lord Himself predicted the dispossession of the Land, the first of which was during the 400 years in Egypt (Gen. 15:13,14). The second prediction is found in Jeremiah 25:11, 12 which Daniel understood as the 70 years in Babylon of which he was a part (Dan. 9:2). These two have been fulfilled, and Israel was restored each time to the Land; but a third prediction of worldwide dispersion is found in Deuteronomy 28:63-68 which details the 19 centuries from A.D. 70 until now. When Israel was legally established as a nation in the Land on May 15, 1948, this third dispossession was not finished. As previously stated, only a partial restoration has been made; but this is certainly a prelude to glorious things to come.

C. Israel's Position in the Land

Israel's existence in the Land has been made rather tenuous as the threat of annihilation has continued to be the war cry of her neighbors. Five wars have evidenced divine providence and preservation. Again this is evidence of the truth of God's Word.

What should you do? What should your government do? We believe God meant what He said when He stated Genesis 12:3 to Abraham. Therefore, our faith in God's Word should be demonstrated and our influence felt by our government representatives. Concern yourself with the Jewish people. Pray for them and their salvation. They are "Jew"-els which the Lord is seeking. Read Psalm 122:6.

Prepare To Discuss Intelligently

1. How can one witness without preaching at the one to whom he is speaking?

2. How are we to understand the injunction of the words "to the Jew first" from Romans 1:16?

3. What is the stone of stumbling and the rock of offense for the Jew as stated in 1 Peter 2:8?

CHAPTER 7

Ecclesiastical Separation and the Apostasy Today

by JOSEPH M. STOWELL, D.D., National Representative of the General Association of Regular Baptist Churches, Des Plaines, IL

BIBLE PORTION TO READ: 2 Corinthians 6:11-18; 7:1

THE BIBLICAL DOCTRINE of separation from the apostasy is an unpopular one. It has ever been so. Whenever a person takes a separated stand, it puts those who do not on the defensive. The nonseparatist often becomes very emotional and sometimes vindictive under such circumstances. We separatists must not react in kind. Like Daniel we must exhibit "an excellent spirit" (Dan. 6:3). As we speak "the truth in love," we must be firm but not bitter (Eph. 4:15).

The separatist must not manifest bigotry nor arrogance. He must courageously yet humbly "contend for the faith which was once delivered unto the saints" (Jude 3).

I. Biblical Background for Separation

The Scriptures indicate that prior to our Lord's

return there will be a great falling away from the faith. This last apostasy will be the greatest. It will culminate in the rule of Antichrist and his false prophet during the Great Tribulation (Rev. 19:20).

In every time of apostasy God preserves a testimony for the truth. He won't be minus a witness in the world. This faithful remnant must separate from the apostasy lest it be infected by its virus of unbelief, lest it be corrupted and contaminated by its manner of life.

We see this principle all through the Bible. The true believer is to recognize the false prophet and turn from such. The truth is kept intact and continues extant in the world by this position of separation.

Among Baptists the application of this was manifest in a great way by that "Prince of Preachers," Charles Haddon Spurgeon (1834-92) of London, England. In his day there came among Baptists a great departure from the faith. Spurgeon called it "The Downgrade Movement." When he saw that the Baptist Union had in it those who denied the faith, he and his church withdrew from the Union.

In the magazine *The Sword and Trowel* Spurgeon wrote, "As soon as I saw, or thought I saw, that error had become firmly established, I did not deliberate, but quitted the body at once. Since then my counsel has been, 'Come out from among them.' I have felt that no protest could be equal to that of separation." Spurgeon set a good example of standing "without the camp" (Heb. 13:13).

The apostasy is upon us. The modern ecumenical movement with its unbelief and crass denial may well be the buildup for the coming world church of the Antichrist.

The Apostle Paul predicted that "in the latter times some shall depart from the faith" (1 Tim. 4:1). The Greek word translated "depart" is the word from which we get our word "apostasy." Christ predicted that before His return many false prophets would arise to deceive, that iniquity would abound and that the love of many would wax cold (Matt. 24:11, 12). Further, He indicated that faith would be scarce on the earth when He came (Luke 18:8). Writing to the church at Thessalonica, Paul stated that the day of the Lord would not come "except there come a falling away first" (2 Thess. 2:3).

The whole matter of separation boils down to the fact that truth and error cannot mix (1 John 4:6). They are poles apart. There is no middle ground between them—only a battleground. There is no peaceful coexistence possible between truth and error. They are eternal enemies. When truth is mixed with error, it ceases to be truth. Modernism is a false religion. The Christ of the liberal is not the Christ of the Bible. The apostate is a false prophet (1 John 4:1-3). A false prophet will deny the truth of the Incarnation. This involves Who Christ is, how He came and why He came.

The false prophet—the apostate—will deny the verbal inspiration of the Scriptures. He will deny one, several or all of five cardinal truths about Christ's person and work. These are: (1) His eternal deity, (2) His virgin birth, (3) His vicarious death by the shedding of blood, (4) His bodily resurrection and (5) His second coming.

II. Biblical View of the Apostasy

The true apostate is a religious person who falsely claims to represent true Christianity. Jesus called such grievous wolves in sheep's clothing (Matt. 7:15; Acts 20:26-32) and "blind leaders of the blind" (Matt. 15:14).

A true, hard-core apostate is a person who knows intellectually the great doctrines of our holy Christian faith. However, he has never believed them nor has he received the Christ they present. He, of course, is not saved. At a given point in time he makes a final, irrevocable decision against the truth. He becomes locked in this position.

Such an individual is under a decreed judgment of God. He cannot be saved. His doom is sealed (Jude 4-7). The apostate cannot be saved.

Further we must understand what the Bible teaches about the true character of the apostate. Not only will he be heretical in doctrine but immoral in practice. We are seeing the apostasy come to its maturity in our day. It has adopted the so-called "new morality" which rejects Biblical absolutism in right and wrong and substitutes humanistic relativism. The apostasy is very vocal in seeking to make homosexuality to be looked upon as a normal way of life. The Bible calls it an abominable sin (Lev. 18:22; 1 Kings 14:24; 1 Cor. 6:9; 1 Tim. 1:9, 10). One cannot avoid the Bible picture of apostasy as having an immoral bent

(Rom. 1:24-28; 2 Tim. 3:6; 2 Pet. 2:18).

In fairness we must point out that many people who are members of apostate churches and organizations are not hard-core apostates. They are just "camp followers." Many are there in ignorance. They can be reached with the gospel.

III. The Biblical Basis of Separation

The apostasy is of such a nature that a true believer cannot be a part of it. That is why our Lord calls, "Come out of her, my people, that ye be not partakers of her sins, and that ye receive not of her plagues" (Rev. 18:4). The apostasy and the true faith are mutually exclusive. The one is the religion of Antichrist—the other of the true Christ.

Paul commanded us not to be unequally yoked with unbelievers (2 Cor. 6:14-18). The believer is righteous; the unbeliever, unrighteous; therefore, there is no basis of fellowship. The born-again one has the light (Ps. 119:130); the unbeliever is in darkness (1 Pet. 2:9). It is written, "Have no fellowship with the unfruitful works of darkness" (Eph. 5:11). The apostasy is of the Devil. How can he that believes consort with an infidel? The true Christian is the temple of God. The apostasy is idolatrous (Hos. 4:17). On the basis of all this we are commanded: "Wherefore come out from among them, and be ye separate, saith the Lord, and touch not the unclean thing; and I will receive you, and will be a Father unto you, and ye shall be my sons and daughters, saith the Lord Almighty" (2 Cor. 6:17, 18).

We are commanded to turn away from the apostasy (2 Tim. 3:5). We are to withdraw from them (1 Tim. 6:5). We are to "avoid them" (Rom. 16:17,

18). We must "have no company with" them (2 Thess. 3:6, 14). The apostate is to be rejected (Titus 3:10). Those who insist on cooperating with Christ-denying modernists help the ungodly in their sinful work (2 Chron. 19:2). We are to let these blind leaders of the blind alone (Matt. 15:14).

Someone says, "I don't think you should be too straitlaced about separation." The Apostle Paul was hard-nosed about a separated stand. He said, "But though we, or an angel from heaven, preach any other gospel unto you than that which we have preached unto you, let him be accursed" (Gal. 1:8). This delineates what our stance should be toward those who preach the social gospel or any other false message!

The Scriptures declare, "The LORD doth put a difference between the Egyptians and Israel" (Exod. 11:7). The Hebrew word translated "difference" means "separation." God draws a line of separation between those who hold the truth and those who hold to error. It is a line fixed by God, not by some fanatical fundamentalist. Therefore we dare not tamper with it. This teaching runs through the whole Bible. God pronounces a woe on pastors who destroy and scatter the sheep of His pasture (Jer. 23:1). This is what the apostate does!

IV. God's Faithful Remnant

God always has a testimony for His truth. Even in the Great Tribulation God will send His two witnesses to herald His truth (Rev. 11:3-12). The faithful remnant stands for the Truth and against apostasy. God has reserved to Himself "seven thousand men, who have not bowed the knee to

the image of Baal" (1 Kings 19:18; Rom. 11:4).
Today there are thousands of fundamental,
separatist Baptist churches. They are standing true
to the Bible and to Christ. They are winning souls,
planting churches and edifying the saints. These
churches are a significant part of God's remnant
today.

The key verse on the subject of the remnant is
Isaiah 1:9. God has placed the remnant in the
world. It is often relatively small compared to the
apostasy. It keeps society from becoming like
Sodom and Gomorrah with their abominable immorality. The mood of society that provides fertile
ground for such gross immorality is described in
Ezekiel 16:49, 50.

God puts the faithful remnant in the world to
raise up a people for His name (Acts 15:14). He
plants local remnant churches, not apostate
churches.

No true believer has a right to belong to an apostate church. He should be active in a fundamental
church. He dare not sit under a false prophet
(Prov. 19:27). He must not be partaker of the apostate's evil deeds (2 John 10, 11). Babes in Christ
must be directed to a fundamental church where
they will get the "milk of the word" and later the
"meat of the word" (1 Cor. 3:2; Heb. 5:13; 1 Pet.
2:2).

V. Neoevangelicalism

Neoevangelicalism, a popular movement today,
militates against the separatist position.

To understand a movement one must know the
purpose of its founding. Dr. Harold John Ockenga, the founder of the movement who also gave it

its name, makes clear its position. When Dr. Ockenga gave his inaugural address as the first president of Fuller Seminary, he said, "We repudiate the come out movement." That, of course, means the separatists. Later in *Christianity Today* (Oct. 10, 1960) he wrote, "The younger orthodox scholars are repudiating the separatist position." In a paper released in 1957 he stated, "The New Evangelicalism has changed its strategy from one of separation to one of infiltration."

In the same release he wrote, "Since I first coined the phrase 'The New Evangelicalism' . . . the evangelical forces have been welded into an organizational front." He then named six parts of this front. "First, the National Association of Evangelicals. Second, the World Evangelical Fellowship. Third, a new apologetic literature stating this point of view. Fourth, the existence of Fuller Seminary and others committed to this view. Fifth, the establishment of *Christianity Today* to articulate the convictions of this movement." Finally he wrote: "Sixth, there is the appearance of an evangelist, Billy Graham, who on the mass level is the spokesman of the convictions and ideals of the New Evangelicalism."

The neoevangelical walks disorderly when he cooperates with unbelievers in Christian work. Therefore we do not cooperate with neoevangelical compromise (2 Thess. 3:6).

Ecumenical evangelism, for example, says that in order to have a successful crusade you have to have liberals, modernists officially serving on the sponsoring committee as well as true believers. To be fair and ethical ecumenical evangelism has to give a percentage of the decision cards to these liberals who help sponsor the crusade. New converts are told, "Go to the church of your choice." This method of evangelism often puts live chicks under dead hens—under false prophets.

A word of warning is due here. We find it in Obadiah 1:11: "In the day that thou stoodest on the other side . . . even thou wast as one of them." This is illustrated in neoevangelicalism. There is a tendency to water down the doctrine of inspiration, eternal punishment and direct creation. Also in the matter of personal separation there is a subtle drift. Some neoevangelicals begin to act like the apostate in such matters as movie attendance, dancing, cocktail drinking and the like.

Many popular religious groups in our day fit in the neoevangelical orbit. World Vision, Campus Crusade and many others fit right here. Key '73 was a movement created by neoevangelical leaders.

VI. Appeal

The remnant deserves the full and loyal support of God's people. This calls for a clean break with the apostasy. It also calls for a refusal to support neoevangelical causes.

We have not yet finished our task of reaching the world with the gospel. It will take our total mobilization with all our resources to get the uncompromised message of the true gospel to all.

Hundreds of fundamental missionary appointees are delayed from going to the field because members of fundamental churches support neoevangelical causes. Separated Christian institutions, schools and local churches are hindered in their work by lack of funds. Anyone who is a convinced fundamentalist and a member of a separated church ought to give the tithe to that local church. In his "over and above" giving he should invest it in fundamental, separated causes. Why "put it into a bag with holes" (Hag. 1:6)?

Prepare To Discuss Intelligently

1. Why do we believe Christ's coming is near?

2. Are there true hard-core apostates alive today? What should be our attitude toward them and the apostasy?

3. Is it proselyting to win a member of a liberal church to Christ and then get that person into a fundamental church?

4. How can we strengthen the churches of the remnant?

CHAPTER 8

The Charismatic Movement

by CHARLES U. WAGNER, D.D., President of North-
west Baptist Seminary, Tacoma, WA

BIBLE PORTIONS TO READ: Acts 2:1-21; 10:34;
18:1—19:7; 1 Corinthians 12:1—15:41

A NYONE casually familiar with present-day
events in professing Christendom will agree
that one problem facing us is that of the charismatic movement. The modern-day tongues movement
touches each of us in our own local situations;
problems are arising daily among Bible-believing
Baptists as to the answers to the charismatic
claims. It is therefore important that we first re-
view the modern-day tongues movement, address-
ing ourselves to the relevancy of the problem as it
exists today, and then attempt to clear up some of
the confusion engendered by the modern-day
tongues movement. Also we will reflect on the
meaning of the true spiritual life as set forth in
Scripture.

I. Tongues Movement Considered Historically

No one would doubt the "speaking in tongues"

in the New Testament. To doubt such would be to doubt God's Word.

Scriptures dealing with tongues are confined to a passage in Mark, several passages in Acts and 1 Corinthians. There is enough material to confirm that tongues existed in the early church and were also a problem to them. The question is not whether tongues were Biblical but whether speaking in tongues is a legitimate gift for our present day.

History seems to confirm that the gift of tongues died out after the canon of the Bible was complete. In *The Modern Tongues Movement* Dr. Robert G. Gromacki gives a historical survey of speaking in tongues in which he concludes (p. 17):

> Therefore, there are no genuine cases of glossolalia in the post-apostolic era. Speaking in tongues had definitely ceased. The testimonies of Justin Martyr, Irenaeus, Origen, Chrysostom and Augustine confirm this conclusion.

In the Middle Ages and Reformation periods the few references to tongues were by those in Roman Catholicism and should be regarded as suspect, especially since there is a propensity on the part of the Roman church to exaggerate various claims of miracles, healings, etc. In the post-Reformation period speaking in tongues was claimed by a number of groups. These were not among those who held orthodox positions in theology but rather linked with the Roman Catholics, Mormons and other groups such as Quakers, Irvingites and Shakers.

Until 1901 there was little or no claim of the gift of tongues by orthodox Christianity. The present-day modern movement could well be considered as having begun in Topeka, Kansas, where Agnes N. Ozman claimed she received the baptism of the Holy Spirit at the Bethel Bible College. The movement spread from Kansas to Missouri and Texas and then eastward. In 1906 the movement came to the Los Angeles area and took on larger proportions. During this time speaking in tongues was confined primarily to Pentecostal groups and was looked upon as being in the "rear ranks of Christendom." The present-day emphasis of the tongues movement affecting churches of a wide variety of denominations did not begin until 1955. It was in the years of 1955 through 1960 that the main thrust of the tongues movement was spearheaded.

Perhaps the organization that has been most responsible for the charismatic movement has been the Full-Gospel Men's Fellowship International. Their techniques have been most helpful in promoting their cause. What is often considered a spontaneous work of the Spirit is in reality the result of clever public relations used by the aggressive body. Aiding in the spreading of the charismatic movement have been the national publications in the secular world, including *Life, Saturday Evening Post, Time, Newsweek*, etc.

The tongues movement has infiltrated various denominations, including Episcopal, Presbyterian and some Baptist bodies (such as the American Baptist Convention and the Southern Baptist Convention). Methodism too has not been free from the growing tongues tide. In fact, every major denominational group has been affected in one way or another by the "tongues people."

No one would doubt that the charismatic movement is "big business," so that large organizations have been formed whose main emphasis is the promotion of glossolalia. Some of these groups include the Christian Growth Ministries, presently in conflict with Oral Roberts; an Episcopal priest, Dennis Bennett; "Mr. Pentecost," David DuPlessis, and national leaders of the Full-Gospel Business Men's Committee International. The late Kathryn Kuhlman was also one of these advocates.

II. Tongues Movement Considered Scripturally

(This is a brief refutation of the modern tongues movement.) It must be understood that the criterion on such a subject as the tongues movement must be God's Word. If we depend on experience, we are on shaky ground. Experience must always be evaluated in the light of the Word of God.

A. The Purpose of Tongues As Revealed in the Scripture

One of the keys in understanding the reason for the tongues movement is found in 1 Corinthians 14:2. Take time to read it. This passage is a quotation from Isaiah 28. An examination of that Old Testament reference will show that God was speaking *to Israel*. God's method of speaking is "with men of other tongues." Paul took the Isaiah passage, explaining the purpose of glossolalia. He continued, "Wherefore tongues are *for a sign,* not to them that believe, but to them that believe not" (1 Cor. 14:22). Here in the heart of this Corinthian passage, Paul gave the key to understanding the movement: *tongues were a sign to the unbelieving Jews.* This writer believes that whenever tongues were used in the Bible, they were used as a sign to the Jews to corroborate the Apostles' message until the canon of Scripture was completed. Each verse dealing with tongues should be examined, looking through the lenses of these important verses.

1. *Acts 2.* At Pentecost the recipients of the message were all Jews (Acts 2:5). There were Jewish people from every nation under Heaven; therefore, they spoke different languages. The purpose of Pentecost was obviously to convey the message of the gospel in their own tongues (v. 8). Not only was it to *convey* the message but to *convince* them through this sign that a new day had come, namely, the inauguration of the Church when God would call out a people for His name from all peoples and nations.

2. *Acts 10:34.* The next mention of tongues is found in the account of the salvation of the house of Cornelius. This might seem to be an exception of the original premise—that tongues were for the Jews—in view of the fact that these were Gentiles; but a closer look at the passage will show that the purpose of the Gentiles speaking in tongues was to *convince the Jews* that "God is no respecter of persons" (Acts 10:34). Later we read, "*And they of the circumcision* which believed were aston-

73

ished, as many as came with Peter, because that on the Gentiles also was poured out the gift of the Holy Ghost" (10:45).

3. *Acts 19:1-7.* A cursory study of this context shows that again we are involved with Jews, many of whom had been recipients of Apollos' ministry (Acts 18:24-28). They were obviously uninformed about the Holy Ghost (19:2) and were disciples of John (19:3). Paul, apparently sensing something lacking in their lives, asked them: "Have ye received the Holy Ghost since ye believed [upon believing]?" They had not so much as heard of the Holy Ghost; so they trusted Christ as Savior, were baptized and spoke in tongues. They were all Jews, unaware of the miracle of Pentecost. It is obvious that tongues were a sign to them and other Jews, for immediately Paul went into the synagogue at Ephesus and ministered there for nine months.

Thus, in all the passages in Acts we find that both the message and the recipient of it are consistent with the Apostle Paul's claim that tongues were a sign to the Jews.

4. *Mark 16:15-18.* While this passage (vv. 9-20) is not in two of the most ancient manuscripts, we refer to it here since tongues were considered a sign.

5. *The Corinthian Passages.* In Corinthians there is the *gift of tongues.* While this difference is obvious, we do not believe that the purpose is changed. It remained a sign to the Jew. In Acts 18 we read that Paul "reasoned *in the synagogue* every sabbath, and persuaded the *Jews* and the Greeks" (vv. 1-4). The church at Corinth began in the house of Justus *located next to the synagogue*

(v. 7). One of the first converts was Crispus, the chief ruler *of the synagogue* who believed with all his heart. While there were some Gentiles, most of the early converts were Jews. Corinth had been considered the "Vanity Fair of the Roman Empire." It was a trade center for business people and merchants from the East and the West. This might have been the reason for the great influx of Jews, known for their financial acumen and business enterprise. It was an ideal place for the Apostle Paul to minister.

B. Temporary Nature of Tongues

Just as we looked to the Corinthian epistle to find the *purpose* of tongues, we also find in chapter 13 the fact of the *cessation* of tongues and the reason. The purpose of 1 Corinthians 13 is to show the superiority of love. In this passage, however, a very important statement is made: "Prophecies . . . shall fail; . . . tongues . . . shall cease; . . . knowledge . . . shall vanish away." (13:8). Here *prophecies* seems to mean a foretelling of the future; *knowledge* indicated supernatural revelational knowledge. Paul also stated that "tongues . . . shall *cease*." Paul spoke of these gifts as having been done away, antiquated, made void, superseded. The time element is also given as to *when* this would be done: "When that which is perfect is come." The word "perfect" is *teleion* which means that which is completed and final.

Paul wrote, "For we know in part, and we prophesy in part" (1 Cor. 13:9). The words "in part" mean "piecemeal," literally "bit by bit." The idea seems to be that through prophecy, supernatural knowledge and tongues, revelation had not been complete, but rather partial. When the perfect Word of God was completed, these temporary gifts would be superseded and no longer be necessary. Some claim that "that which is perfect" refers to the coming of Christ. However, it cannot be the Second Coming, as the neuter in the Greek denotes that it is "something" not "someone." Also, every reference to Christ's coming is in the masculine. Again, another reason that it cannot be His Second Coming is that prophecy will not cease at the Rapture; there will be much prophecy during the Tribulation (Rev. 11) and during the Millennium (Joel 2:28).

Clearly, then, that "which is perfect" seems to be the completion of the canon of Scripture. This is also confirmed by the fact that in the later epistles of Paul when the gifts are mentioned (Rom. 12; Eph. 4) the sign-gifts of tongues have been omitted. Again history confirms this as we have stated earlier. In the early church after the completion of the canon there were no references to speaking in tongues except those who were heretical. Tongues, then, were a sign to the Jew to corroborate the Word of God until the completion of the canon of the Scripture. Then, in accordance with Scripture, they ceased.

III. Tongues Movement Considered Ecclesiastically

We will now look at the tongues movement as it affects the local church.

A. The Tongues Movement Is Divisive

It is safe to say that thousands of churches have been affected by the tongues movement. Many of them have been split. The modern-day tongues movement is not a unifying one. Rather, it is a tool being used to divide and fragment many precious congregations.

B. The Tongues Movement Is Deceptive

Often people who speak in tongues have distorted views of the meaning of true spirituality. They have a "superiority complex"; their view of the spiritual life is not in bearing the fruit of the Spirit but in the *experience* of tongues. Thus they have deceived themselves of the true meaning of spirituality as well as the members of the congregation. The pseudo-spiritual complexion of the tongues movement is deceptive.

C. The Tongues Movement Is Diverting

In areas where the tongues movement prevails there is an emphasis on *experience* as opposed to God's Word. The very purpose of the ministry of the Holy Spirit is to cause our focus to be on Christ (John 16:13, 14).

D. The Tongues Movement Is Dangerous

Many have attempted to explain the modern-day tongues movement. People often ask for an explanation of the growth of the tongues movement. There is little doubt in the writer's mind that much of it is a result of demon work. The Bible makes clear that in the latter times "some shall depart from the faith, giving heed to seducing spirits, and doctrines of devils [demons]" (1 Tim. 4:1).

Conclusion

A consideration of tongues in history shows that

there was no Scriptural tongues movement in the early postapostolic period, that it was confined primarily to heretics until the nineteenth or twentieth century and even then was practiced by fringe groups until its most recent modern surge. Considered Scripturally, it has been noted that tongues are a temporary gift and specifically a sign to the Jew until the completion of the canon. Its effect on the church is divisive, deceptive and diverting; and it also has many attendant dangers.

Prepare To Discuss Intelligently

1. What are the reasons for the upsurge in the charismatic movement today?

2. How far should a church go in allowing the "tongues viewpoint" to be presented in the church?

3. What are the effects of a position that is "soft" regarding the movement?

4. What are some inconsistencies in the movement, and how is the movement different today from the one in the early church?

CHAPTER 9

Demons in Today's World

by RALPH G. COLAS, Pastor of South Holly Baptist
Church, Littleton, CO

BIBLE PORTIONS TO READ: 2 Corinthians 2:11;
Ephesians 6:10-18; 2 Timothy 2:25, 26; 1 Peter
5:8, 9

THE FILM *The Exorcist* has been the
biggest thing to hit Hollywood in years. There
is no doubt that it will surpass the record of $150
million income which was reached by the film *The
Godfather*. About $14 million was spent in its pro-
duction.

Why would people stand in line for hours to see
a shocking film that causes many to faint and become violently ill? The media tells us that a person
would have to be a block of wood not to be
shocked by the spectacle of a child turned into a
yellow-eyed, slime-spewing, head-swiveling mon-
ster. Dr. Z. Lebensohn, an outstanding psychiatrist
of Washington, D.C., said: "The overwhelming
popularity of this movie points up the tremendous
lack in many people's lives. They have a need for
some type of moving emotional experience."

The interest in the subjects of demons and exorcism is not restricted to the patrons of this Warner Brothers production or to those who purchased the 9 million copies of William Blatty's *The Exorcist*. Among the most popular subjects in religious writing today is that of the occult. An unhealthy interest in demons and exorcism is spreading like wildfire. While some may call it a fad, the evidence shows it to be stepped-up satanic activity.

I. The Occult

A. The Definition

The "occult" is defined as that which is "related to supernatural agencies, their effects and knowledge of them." It is derived from the Latin word *occultus* meaning "hidden, secret, dark and concealed." It is used to describe those phenomena which transcend or seem to transcend the world of the five senses.

B. The Demons

Liberal teachers deny the reality of demons and suggest they are only a myth and a figment of the imagination. Some even teach that Jesus Christ accommodated Himself to the ignorance of people of His time. In other words, He knew there were no demons but went along with the ignorance of His day. Such heretical teaching makes our Savior a deceiver and a sinner, neither of which is true.

Both the Old and New Testaments abound with material on the subject at hand. The Bible declares that demons are real spirit personalities whose origin is not revealed but who are under Satan's control. These supernatural beings are numerous. In one person (Mark 5:9) they were called "legion." If the Roman legion is the number in view, this would be at least 6,000. In their departure from the Gadarene man, they invaded and destroyed 2,000 swine (Mark 5:13).

C. The Distinct Characteristics

Demons desire to possess and indwell bodies of others—men, children and beasts (Matt. 8:28, 32; Mark 9:21). These spirit beings have the ability to speak and even possess unusual knowledge of future events (Matt. 8:29; Acts 16:16).

Those demon-possessed individuals in the New Testament were lonely, possessing great strength, lacking in modesty and had self-destructive tendencies.

II. The Obsession

A recent check at a Christian bookstore revealed almost two dozen books on spiritism, Satanism, mysticism, witchcraft, demons and exorcism. Most of these books were beautifully designed with eye-catching covers and intriguing titles. They were being marketed by popular Christian publishing houses.

There is a preoccupation with the occult, demons and Satanism prevalent that can produce powerless, depressed and emotionally upset Christians. Those who have done research on emotional depression have discovered that people who have a veritable interest and occupation in the study of and interest in these things can experience periods of depression in direct proportion to their involvement. Even the reading of current books on the subject of the occult tends to leave the believer with a depressed feeling, robbing him of joy.

A. Exorcism

In recent months a disturbing practice has appeared prominently among some so-called evangelical groups. It is the supposed act of casting out demons from believers. In such meetings, hundreds of sincere (but untaught) people are encouraged to submit to exorcism for the demons of fear, lying, blasphemy, cancer, discouragement and pride. Numbers of such "demons" are "discerned" in these individuals. They are told to "spit up demoniac substances" in dramatic "deliverance services."

The Bible teaches us that Jesus Christ practiced exorcism. The Lord's disciples and Philip and Paul also did so but in a limited sense. There is no Scripture indicating this to be a proper and Scriptural ministry for today's believers. The church or pastoral epistles do not support the practice of casting demons out of anyone. For one to build a doctrine today that calls for exorcism, apart from the direct command of God's Word, can bring only confusion among the Lord's followers.

The silence of Scripture is not without significance. As the late Dr. M. R. DeHaan declared, "Where the Scriptures are silent, it is for us to keep silent." Twenty-one New Testament books given "for doctrine, for reproof, for correction, for instruction in righteousness" (2 Tim. 3:16), with the purpose of maturing believers (v. 17), remain basically silent regarding casting out demons. This silence is more than accidental!

Those who believe in the practice of exorcism might be asked to consider questions like these: (1) How do we recognize demons? (2) How can someone differentiate between what is the direct work of the Devil and demon-possession? (3) To what extent is the pollution of the Adamic nature and the work of the flesh seen? (4) Can neurotic or psychotic behavior possibly be mistaken for demon possession? (5) Is exorcism a part of the Great Commission?

Some of those who have now "set up shop" and entered the "Demon Removal Ministry" are Christian laymen and ministers who are actively engaged in "casting demons" out of other Christians as well as the unsaved. The extreme to which this can lead is illustrated by one minister who publicly said that before he went into a local church to preach, he would first cast out all the demons in the building. He would, in the name of Christ, exorcise such demons as "baby-pincher," "distracter," etc., and even cast out the demons in the pictures in the nursery! What a statement!

B. Experiential Evidence

There is a serious danger in making experience the foundational stone of any doctrine. A well-known Bible teacher, who once taught that a born-again believer could not be demon-possessed, has now changed his view. In correspondence with this writer he explained that he had altered his former position because it was "not in accord with authenticated experience." Note that it was because of experiential evidence rather than the Scriptures. This teacher may have forgotten an important dictum: *We test our experience by the Word of God!* As subjective creatures we must accept the objective truths of God's Word rather than phenomena witnessed even by some very reliable individuals.

III. The Overcomers

A battle rages! Spiritism, demonism and other forms of supernaturalism whose activity is on the increase can serve as a reminder that these are the last days. A glance at the yellow pages of the telephone directories of many cities reveals a large number of occult bookstores. These stores sell everything from books on black and white magic to witchcraft. Public libraries report that many are showing a keen interest in books on the occult. In one year alone Americans purchased 2 million Ouija boards.

This stepped-up tempo is the normal product of a society which has rejected divine authority. The omission and open rejection of God's Word in our educational system has prepared the soil for the enemy's tares. Public schools now teach "approved" courses in the occult at taxpayer's expense. Television programs have made witchcraft intriguing and popular until occult concepts are accepted as normal or even desirable.

Paul spoke of "perilous times" which would characterize the last days. Interestingly, this same word is also used in Matthew 8:28 to describe the demoniac of Gadara who was "exceeding fierce."

A cursory glance at our world today reveals the same kind of rejection of authority, emotional and mental instability along with shamelessness that was the conduct of this man of Gadara.

Believers themselves may be deceived because they are not properly equipped for this warfare or possibly not knowledgeable concerning their provisions from the Lord.

A. The Protection

A defeat in our lives may come because of carelessness of life and failure to keep our eyes on Christ, our Source of power and victory.

A word of warning should be sounded about a continual study of the occult. Such a practice can render us both powerless and fruitless. An effective tool in our personal work is the abundant life of joy which our lovely Lord gives His children (John 10:10). That dynamic life never results from feeding on the occult, but by being filled with the Holy Spirit Who fills the believer's mind with Christ's glory.

Nowhere in the Bible are we admonished to spend excessive amounts of time studying our enemy and his techniques. We are not to be "ignorant of his devices" (2 Cor. 2:11), but to major on the subject can be detrimental to us.

Believers must be able to recognize that Satan and the occult are our enemies and should be kept at arm's length. The Lord has provided a way for us to be strong and to overcome the wicked one (1 John 2:14). The child of God should inspect and use his spiritual armor (Eph. 6:10-18).

B. The Provisions

In these times of increased demonic activity believers, both spiritual babes and long-standing saints, must be instructed in their provisions. Spiritual pastors and teachers must exercise loving care in a watchful oversight, ever sensitive to the tactics of the enemy. At the same time they should be providing a health-stimulating, nutritional diet for the flock.

The child of God must remember that while our enemy never sleeps, rests or takes a vacation, neither does the Lord Jesus Christ, our High Priest, for one moment cease His interceding in our behalf (Heb. 7:25). Every believer has a share in Christ's priestly work and can come boldly to the throne of grace in time of need (Heb. 4:16).

Here are some practical suggestions to make us overcomers:

1. Confess and forsake all sin. Sin permits Satan to gain a foothold in one's life (Eph. 4:27).

2. Read God's Word daily (Ps. 1:2). We need to feed our souls regularly from God's Word. We will not be strong physically without eating, and it is the same spiritually. We must saturate our minds with the Bible (Rom. 12:2).

3. Be continually "filled with the Spirit" (Eph. 5:18-21). A Spirit-filled Christian with a song in his heart, a thankful attitude and a spirit of submission to God's will is better prepared to face the enemy's attacks.

4. The Apostle Peter told us to consciously resist the Devil (1 Pet. 5:8, 9). This includes rejecting all practices relating to the occult and Satan's toys—staying clear of the horoscope, palmistry, seances, fortune telling, the Ouija boards and related practices.

C. The Promises

Our Lord has given us precious promises that assure us of victory. We would encourage you to read thoughtfully the following verses and commit them to memory: Romans 8:31; Hebrews 2:14, 15; 1 John 3:8 and 4:4.

Prepare To Discuss Intelligently

1. Are there "good" demons and "bad" demons?

2. Can a Christian be demon-possessed?

3. A popular TV comic has the line, "The Devil made me do it." Is this damaging?

4. What are some side effects from seeing *The Exorcist* or reading such books?

CHAPTER 10

Your Body and You

by DAVID NETTLETON, D.D., President of Faith Baptist Bible College, Ankeny, IA

BIBLE PORTION TO READ: 1 Corinthians 12:1—15:58

BELOVED, I wish above all things that thou mayest prosper and be in health, even as thy soul prospereth" (3 John 2).

There is a vain philosophy that considers all material things evil. Some view the soul as spiritual and therefore to be given careful attention, but they think the body to be mere matter— mortal and evil, undeserving of care.

The soul is more important than the body; that is true. However, that does not make the body unimportant and insignificant. While some consider the body to be evil, others make a religion out of caring for the body. Neither extreme is correct. The body is the creation of God and a temple of the soul. We owe our bodies great care and sacred use.

I. The Body—Its Creation

A. God's Special Creation

Thoughtfully read Genesis 1:26 and 27. These verses reveal the noble purpose of man. He was created in God's image to show forth God's glory in a most special way. Man was to have dominion "over all the earth" and was created for God alone.

The false theory of evolution, stating that man evolved from lower forms of life, contradicts God's Word. Evolution cannot be proven. It is not our purpose to array lengthy and complicated arguments against the theory of evolution. However, note a suggestion or two in passing. A main argument of evolutionists is that of similarity of structure. Man's body is like the general structure of the body of the lower forms of animals, and all have some similarity in cellular structure. This only proves that animals and man came from the same source. Similarity and diversity are both mentioned—diversity in that both man and animals reproduce only "after their kind." There are links of similarity, yet walls of separation. That is the way God set it up. Starting with the same facts, some conclude it was evolution while others believe in creation. But we can never fully evaluate man and the human body until we believe it is the product of an all-wise mind and God's skillful hand, and that it was especially made for the soul— to serve as a temple also of the Holy Spirit.

B. Fearfully and Wonderfully Made

Read Psalm 139:14 and 15. Were it not for the curse due to sin, the human body would not die.

Death isn't the normal experience; it is the result of sin. Even with the curse upon us, the wonders of the human body stand out. In the last fifty years more and more doctors have specialized in one or several organs of the body. Each is becoming a lifetime study in itself—"fearfully and wonderfully made."

Each organ is a wonder in itself, and the harmony with which the organs work together is beyond our comprehension. There is the nervous system (our electrical system with which we are wired); it activates the muscles and also carries back messages of pain and strain to the brain. At the center of it all is the heart, supplying blood and nourishment to all the body. It beats on and on. This muscular pump of ours performs enough work every twenty-four hours to lift a weight of ten to fifteen tons to a height of five to six feet; and it keeps this up day after day, year after year, resting only between beats.

Consider also the healing qualities of the body. Blood is so constituted that it clots and healing sets in. A broken bone has the ability to knit back together again and be usable.

The eyes, ears, nose and skin act as protectors, sensing danger and sending signals to the brain which in turn reasons a way out.

No sweeter musical instrument was ever

fashioned than the human voice which is capable of such a variety of tones and also can sound out the words and the message with meaning.

The human body is the crowning act of God's creation.

II. The Body—Its Care

Read 1 Corinthians 10:31. This verse was written to answer some moral actions of the body, but it also has physical implications.

God provided for the body. He gave man food and drink. He clothed the body to cover shame and to protect it. He provided night for the body's rest. But man abuses his body terribly and pays a great price for abuse and neglect.

Since the body isn't our own (1 Cor. 6:19), we must avoid abuses; and this isn't easy. Some of these subjects are very "touchy," but let us not be easily offended.

One other caution: It isn't wise to make a religion out of body care. Avoid extremes in dieting and exercise. Sift theories carefully (1 Thess. 5:21).

A. Care of the Respiratory System

1. *Fresh Air Necessary*. Lots of good fresh air is a tonic to the body. We spend only a small fraction of our time outdoors. The older we get, the more we neglect this, especially in unpleasant weather. Enjoy outdoor activities.

2. *Avoid Smoking. Dangers:* It is a well-proven fact that tobacco smoking, especially of cigarettes, is related to lung cancer, a painful killer. Thousands each year are victims of it. Emphysema and heart trouble are also related to smoking. How

does 1 Corinthians 6:19, 20 apply to this?

According to a recent report, Sweden has set a goal of rearing a generation of nonsmokers. The World Health Organization reported that in 1970 cigarette consumption among the 8 million Swedes averaged 1,620 per person. Compare that year's statistics with other countries:

Americans	3,670
British	over 3,000
Germans	2,500
Frenchmen	1,830
Norwegians	1,760

The Swedes have the longest life expectancy of any nation—seventy-two for men and seventy-seven for women. Their main weapon against tobacco is an educational one. They also benefit from having no local tobacco production.

Smoking can cost between $140 and $250 per year per person. In 50 years that could mean a minimum of $7,000. This amount of money put into a savings account could amount to over $17,000 and could yield over $100 a month at retirement instead of the torture of lung cancer.

There is a way out (Rom. 8:13). Note "*through the Spirit.*" Help from God through prayer is the only answer. God promised to help.

B. Care of the Digestive System

Hogs, poultry and cattle are fed most scientifically. Compare that to the way many human beings are fed. The Christian owes it to himself to control what enters his mouth.

1. *Alcohol.* Some Christians are taking a soft line on wine and beer and even on whiskey. (Read Romans 12:2.) How can one know how far this

might lead? Otherwise strong people have become alcoholics. The only safe course is *total abstinence*.

2. *Gluttony* (Prov. 23:2). One is tempted to ignore this part of the study, but the problem is so common and far-reaching that we must consider it.

A smoking man said to an overweight man, "You are harming your body by your overweight more than I am harming mine by my smoking." Doctors and insurance companies agree that overweight is dangerous.

Consider the consequences of gluttony as it leads to overweight. It affects one's general health. It can shorten life because of strain on the heart. A surplus of fat outside the body indicates a coating of fat on the internal organs of the body, slowing down their functions.

Overweight affects one's social and family life. When a person becomes so unattractive from excessive weight, it affects both.

Overweight affects a person's working life. Often one's work speed is lessened, and he cannot enjoy physical work.

Enjoyable and profitable athletic activities are impossible or inconvenient for the overweight person. Enjoyment of life can be narrowed significantly due to this same problem.

Consider the result of one's loss of self-respect. Many are ashamed of their eating habits.

Since the body is the Lord's temple, we must care for it and keep it in shape. Self-control is one facet of the fruit of the Spirit. Such should apply to the habit of eating.

In a very real sense overeating can be considered a *spiritual* problem where the Bible and prayer enter in. Periodic fasting, prayer, reading of appropriate Bible passages, careful living habits, avoidance of fad temporary diets, plenty of sensible exercise and the establishing of normal eating habits can all combine to curb the appetite, return the weight to normal and bring health and happiness. Make it a spiritual challenge and "do thyself no harm" (Acts 16:28).

Sensible dieting for general health is commendable even when there is no problem. A study of nutrition is in order for all, and many good books are available. May God give us grace to be sensible in this matter. Do not eat that for which you cannot sincerely thank God.

C. Care of the Nervous System

Read Proverbs 13:12 and 17:22. The mind not only affects the body; it is a part of it. Hence worry or wrong attitudes in life can affect one's health. God's peace (Phil. 4:7) and joy are boons to well-being.

An earnest Christian once worked two jobs and was so busy that he averaged four hours of sleep each night. It was telling on his entire physical condition. His eyes and face showed wear and strain. An unbeliever, whom he had rebuked for destroying his health by smoking, looked him in the eye one day and said, "You are hurting your body worse than I'm hurting mine." The Christian went back to regular hours of sleep. It wasn't right to destroy his nervous system by lack of sleep.

In our day of mind-altering drugs much has been written on the dangers of drugs. Much should be written on the good effect of prayer.

D. Care of the Muscular System

Is there such a thing as vigorous health without

exercise? I think not. We live artificial lives sitting behind desks or at a machine. In order to counteract this, all kinds of recreation are practiced and a great variety of exercising machines are being sold. We must exercise to keep the muscles firm, the lungs working and the heart strong.

Long walks in the open air are the best and most natural way to care for the body's muscles and organs. Dr. Paul Dudley White, physician to one of America's great Presidents, said, "My heart has two friends—my right leg and my left leg."

E. Care of the Circulatory System

Train the heart, but don't strain it. Moderation is the watchword.

A noted medical doctor and author suggests seven prescriptions for better health:

1. Exercise—to be active is to live.

2. Abstain from nicotine—smoking invites early coronary disease, emphysema, lung cancer and chronic cough from chemical bronchitis.

3. Abstain from alcohol—it contributes to crime as well as disease.

4. Do not become overweight—reducing is a form of discipleship.

5. Limit animal fats in the diet—animal fat was forbidden under Jewish law (Lev. 7).

6. Reduce salt intake—heavy salt intake contributes to hypertension.

7. Avoid fatigues and stress—walking relaxes tension. So does prayer.

— from *Physician to Pastor. Golf Isn't Enough* by A. D. Dennison Jr., who holds the M.D. from Cornell University Medical College, is a fellow of the American College of Physicians and is the author of about fifty publications in the medical and religious fields.

III. The Body—Its Use

Slowly read Romans 6:12, 13, 19b and 12:1. Let those phrases linger in your mind and thus ennoble the body and its use: "instruments of righteousness," "—servants to righteousness unto holiness."

A. Holiness

"Unto holiness." Here again read thoughtfully 1 Corinthians 6:15, 18 and 20.

First Corinthians 6 pictures the transforming view of the body's use. Paul writes of fornicators, idolaters, adulterers, effeminate, abusers, thieves, covetous and drunkards and others; and he says, "Such were some of you: but ye are washed . . . sanctified . . . justified" (1 Cor. 6:11). It proceeds from this to show the sacredness of the human body and concludes with "glorify God in your body."

The worldly way of life is destructive to the body, but the spiritual way regards the body as a member of Christ to be used for His glory.

B. A Living Sacrifice

"Present your bodies a living sacrifice" (Rom. 12:1). Christ calls us to offer our bodies for His service.

1. *Contrast.* The word "sacrifice" usually denoted an altar and a dead animal. In the human realm it might suggest a martyr such as Stephen (Acts 7) who laid down his life as a sacrifice. In Romans 12 Paul wrote about a "*living* sacrifice."

It is an act of supreme dedication when one dares to die for the sake of the Lord Jesus. But a life lived as a "living sacrifice" is an entirely different matter, for it calls for continuing action, continual suffering and continual sacrifice.

2. *Service.* "Which is your reasonable service." Now we come to the true purpose of our bodies. We care for them because they are God's property, but we care for them so they will be strong, clean and fit for service (Rom. 10:15; Isa. 52:7).

As Paul served in his body, he suffered in his body for the Lord Jesus (Gal. 6:17). Surely such suffering is part of what Paul meant when he wrote, "Glorify God in your body" (1 Cor. 6:20).

Prepare To Discuss Intelligently

1. What does similarity of structure in animals suggest?

2. How do you answer the smoker who says, "I'm not hurting anyone but myself"?

3. How can the Scriptures help in dieting?

4. What does Paul call the body in 1 Corinthians 6:19?

CHAPTER 11

Alcohol—Our National Blight

by HARRY ZEMMER, M.D., Physician and Former
Missionary to Africa, Lapeer, MI

BIBLE PORTION TO READ: Proverbs 23:20-34

THE JAPANESE SAY, "A man takes a drink,
and the drink takes a drink, and the next drink
takes the man."

"Intoxicating drinks have produced evils more
deadly, because more continuous, than all those
caused to mankind by the great historic scourges
of war, famine and pestilence combined"—
Gladstone.

The Bible is not silent concerning any force
which ruins men's souls. It strikes hard against all
Satan's tricks and devices, and it clearly denun-
ciates drunkenness.

I. Reason

Warnings against the use of fermented drink have
come down to us in the earliest sacred and secular
writings.

A. Physical

1. *Mechanism of Action*. The result of alcoholic

98

fermentation is ethyl alcohol, one of a family of alcohol poisons, two of which—methyl and ethyl—are better known. The two members of this family resemble two members of the same human families in that while the names look alike and sound alike, they behave differently. Methyl alcohol, when taken into the blood stream, has a peculiar affinity for the optic nerve, causing blindness if not death. Ethyl alcohol affects the whole nervous system, causing all its functions to be less acute and active. The latter is more dangerous but not nearly so startling to the drinker.

Alcohol is one substance that is taken directly into the blood stream in the very form in which it is eaten. When alcohol is taken into the stomach, 20 percent is absorbed directly into the bloodstream from the stomach and 80 percent in the intestinal tract. The alcohol is then metabolized by the liver at the rate of one-third ounce per hour. If alcohol is being consumed at a faster rate than this, it builds up in the bloodstream. The alcohol in the stomach will continue to be absorbed even after the person has become unconscious. This accounts for the fact that when a person has had many drinks quickly and has become unconscious, often this person is found dead at a later time because the amount of alcohol being absorbed into the bloodstream was at a higher rate than it was being detoxified, and the level of alcohol in the blood became high enough to kill the person.

The observances of physicians in the controlled laboratory experiments of scientists with alcohol have been carefully reported and the effects may be classified under four general heads: (a) It is a narcotic. As such it exerts its first and most serious effect on the nervous system and the functions of seeing, feeling, moving, thinking, self-control, etc., by numbing them and thereby making them less acute and active. (b) It is a deterrent of important bodily functions. It hinders and slows down the actions of glands and organs, thereby delaying their actions and causing overwork of these agencies, resulting in degenerations and disease because of injury to cells. (c) It is a habit-forming drug, tending to create a desire for its effects which, because of the numbing action, is each time the less readily resisted. (d) It is a poison which attacks the protoplasm in the body cells in life germ cells, thus affecting important organs and endangering the offspring.

2. *Mental.* After drinking, the drinker sees less clearly, feels less acutely and thinks less keenly because alcohol affects the nerves before affecting the muscular action. It is less well known, but just as true, that alcohol also affects reason, judgment and self-control, the highest functions of the human mind. These functions—ambition, enthusiasm, will, conscience, bravery, reason, judgment, love and self-control—make man different from and superior to animals. These functions of thinking are all subject to control; but when the highest power is impaired, the others degenerate from the desirable to the undesirable: Bravery

without control becomes riot; love without control becomes lustful passion.

3. *Malfunction of the Body.* A research team at Brown University reported: "Eight volunteers were tested before and after drinking enough to bring their blood alcohol levels to .08 percent. The results: Average reaction time was slowed by 25 percent; 20 percent reduction in muscle strength."

A report of "Fetal Alcohol Syndrome" in the *Journal of the American Medical Association* (referred to hereafter as JAMA) of June 16, 1975, by Margaret Tenbrinck, M.D.: "The association between maternal alcoholism and faulty development of offspring has been suspected since antiquity. This syndrome is marked by low birthweight and delayed growth and development. These defects are not corrected despite attempts at optimum nutrition. Additional features are deformed skull, large ears, flattened nose, eyes slanting down and laterally, mouth turned down at the corners, and delayed bone age."

B. Economics

1. *Poor Health.* "Alcohol is this country's number one health problem" (*Insight,* Flint, Michigan). From the *Post Graduate Medical Journal,* January, 1973, page 101, we read, "It is estimated that there are 10 million alcoholics in the United States and that 25 percent of all general hospital admissions relate to medical compensation resulting from the excessive use of alcohol."

Alcohol is a depraver (Prov. 23:29-35). Liquor destroys (Prov. 23:29, 30). This is true morally, mentally, physically and spiritually. Red eyes, wounds, headaches—these are only outward signs of the more serious inward physical destruction of alcohol. Then woe and sorrow speak of mental and social distress. Moral and spiritual destruction always follows.

2. *Production Loss.* From the *U.S. News and World Report* of July 15, 1974: "The heavy drinker is a major labor problem for American industry—one that costs 15 billion dollars a year. Some 5 million alcoholics are still on the job. The National Council on Alcoholism figures that each problem drinker costs his employer on the average of three thousand dollars a year in sick pay, accidents, lost production and, especially in the case of executives, bad judgment."

3. *Poverty.* American consumers spent an average of more than 3.1 million dollars an hour on alcoholic beverages last year, for a staggering total of 27.2 billion dollars. Alcohol figures in 800,000 traffic accidents a year, including half of the fatal ones. Total consumption of alcoholic beverages at retail prices equals 15 billion dollars per year.

C. Moral

1. *Family Breakup.* Drunkenness is related to immorality and sin (Rom. 13:13). Not only does drunkenness dull the mind and depress the spirit, but it inflames the baser passions and brings out the animal in man. One expert authority estimates that 50 percent of the divorces in America are the result of or related to drunkenness.

Alcohol and juvenile delinquency go hand in hand. It is reported that three of five cases of juvenile delinquency come from homes where the parents drink.

2. *Frustrated Children*. The Department of Mental Health Services, the Board of Education and Hunter College collaborated on a study of 10,000 high school students in ninety-one schools in New York. The results indicated that as many as 12 percent of the juniors and seniors were alcoholics and 80 percent of the students drank alcoholic beverages.

3. *Futile Living*. While the school may be concerned about pollution of the environment, Dr. C. A. Hoffman, past president of the American Medical Association, asked about the teenager who comes to school hung over from the beer bust the night before. He declared, "It is high time to do something about this personal pollution." He estimates that 6 percent of America's teenagers will become alcoholics."

D. Spiritual

1. *Depraved Nature (Matt. 24:45-51)*. The contrast in these verses is between the good servant who recognized that his one and constant obligation was to serve whether his master was present or absent, and the evil servant who violated his trust. Notice that his first thought after harsh treatment of his fellow servants was to satisfy his appetite—to "drink with the drunken."

Cruelty, mismanagement and unfaithfulness are tied up with drinking. The final result of the servant in our Scripture text was the loss of his position and his life.

2. *Departure from Scripture*. This is a very serious matter. Scripture is explicit about the Christian's need to abstain from alcohol. The weak,

expedient argument for temperance instead of abstinence is not valid.

3. *Desire for Flesh*. Drunkenness is not a disease; it is a vicious, ugly, devastating sin (1 Cor. 6:10). Without God man's heart is an empty vacuum. He tries to fill that vacuum with things other than God. He substitutes pleasure, lust, drunkenness, revelings and wantonness; but he cannot fill that void without Christ.

II. Remedy

A. Negative

1. *Social*. Mr. James S. Kemper, Jr., President of Kemper Insurance and Financial Companies, said, "The things you would think would motivate some to quit drinking—pride, family, reputation in the community—don't work" (*U.S. News and World Report*, July 15, 1974).

2. *Legal*. The Committee on Alcoholism and Drug Dependence reported in the *JAMA*, May 10, 1971: "In the main, effectual social response to the abuse of alcohol lies in areas other than legal control."

3. *Education*. The Committee on Alcoholism and Drug Dependence reported in the *JAMA*, May 10, 1971: "Education on alcohol's various aspects—its physiological, psychological and social implications and effects—could help develop a more circumspect public attitude on drinking. Community education programs can play an important role." Visits to centers for treatment of alcoholics, dissemination of statistics on home and auto accidents involving drinkers, and meetings with A. A. (Alcoholics Anonymous) are no cure.

4. *Alcoholics Anonymous.* Few of us realize what A. A. really believes. Let me quote from the *Guide to the Twelve Steps of Alcoholics Anonymous,* second step:

> Many tried doctors and hospitals. Some of us tried religion. We found deep sympathy, but we did not find sobriety. The results were always the same—we got drunk again. Willpower, help from families and friends, medicine, formal religion having failed, there is but one place to turn. *That is to God as we understand Him.* This is not as difficult as it might seem. *You are not asked to go to church. You are not asked to seek the advice of a clergyman.* You are only asked to quit trying to run your own life, and to keep an open mind. You are asked to accept the teaching from a group of men who have ironed out the problem that is bringing you deep trouble.

B. Positive

1. *Salvation.* The person who receives Jesus Christ as Savior by believing in Him is born again (John 1:12; 3:16, 36; Prov. 29:25). He is thus freed from sin's bondage and slavery (Rom. 6:6, 7).

Notice the shout of victory over the appetites of the flesh found in Romans 6:22.

2. *Spiritual Growth—Bible Grounds for Opposing Liquor.*

a. The Bible requires total abstinence. Children of Israel drank no wine nor strong drink for forty years during the wilderness wandering. God commanded the priests to drink neither wine nor strong drink (Lev. 10:8, 9). God commanded the Nazarites to drink no wine or strong drink (Num. 6:1-3). God commanded the mother of Samson to drink no wine or strong drink (Judg. 13:4-14). Samson, being a Nazarite, was a total abstainer. Samuel, the great judge of Israel, was a total abstainer. Daniel, the great prophet, was a total abstainer who purposed in his heart he would not defile himself with the king's meat nor with the wine which he drank (Dan. 1:8). John the Baptist, the forerunner of Jesus, was a total abstainer (Luke 1:15). Paul, the great apostle to the Gentiles, wrote, "It is good neither to eat flesh, nor to drink wine, nor any thing whereby thy brother stumbleth, or is offended, or is made weak" (Rom. 14:21). In 1 Corinthians 5 and 6 and Galatians 5 Paul wrote a category of the lust of the flesh. In all three categories he listed drunkenness along with murder, stealing, adultery and fornication, idolatry and other sins of the flesh. Now what does the Bible say we ought to do with the lusts of the flesh? "Abstain from fleshly lusts, which war against the soul" (1 Pet. 2:11).

b. The Bible records tragedy growing out of strong drink. Noah was hardly out of the ark before he was lying naked and drunk before his family. Lot's two daughters—barely out of Sodom—made their father drunk and lay in adultery with him. David tried to cover his own adultery by getting Uriah drunk. Handsome Absalom made his half brother drunk so that he could slay him with a sword. John the Baptist got his head cut off at a drunken birthday dance.

c. The Bible warns against strong drink. "Woe unto him that giveth his neighbour drink" (Hab. 2:15). "Wine is a mocker, strong drink is raging: and whosoever is deceived thereby is not wise" (Prov. 20:1). (See also Isaiah 5:11, 22, 23; Proverbs 23:29-33; 31:4 and 5.)

Prepare To Discuss Intelligently

1. From a strictly secular standpoint why should one avoid the use of alcohol?

2. What Scriptures would you use in speaking with a person about his need to abstain from the use of alcohol?

3. What would you do to help a person to see the danger of so-called social drinking?

CHAPTER 12

Missions at This Hour

by WENDELL W. KEMPTON, D.D., President of Association of Baptists for World Evangelism, Cherry Hill, NJ

BIBLE PORTION TO READ: Acts 1:1—7:60

THIS GLOBAL VILLAGE called planet earth has undergone severe cataclysmic change since World War II. The continued world move toward urbanization, the sensational growth of population and the constant rise of nationalism have forced changes which seem to have left the people dizzy, stunned and numb. Since World War II there have been over fifty wars. From 1960 on, over forty countries have achieved independence while world population has broken all records with 250,000 more people daily.

No one knows how to stop this merry-go-round. It keeps gaining speed, forcing people of the world to change in a direction which appears contrary to their nature and culture. All over the world, people are talking about freedom, peace, love and happiness. Where is this whole thing leading? These are interesting questions that deserve answers.

In the midst of all this change the Church of Jesus Christ has existed as a unique entity. However, the Lord's Body also has experienced turbulent weather which has left her seeking the proper future course of direction. Some critics say that the Christian ship of grace is out of sight and will never return to the harbor. This author repudiates this position and acclaims that the Lord and His true Church *are* on course and will be until the Rapture.

Through the centuries the Church's true temperature could be detected by its response to its responsibilities. This is especially true when it came to taking Christ to the world.

I. The Church's Mandate

Perhaps the most quoted New Testament text outside of John 3:16 is Matthew 28:19, 20. Our Lord commissioned His Church with an order which is still contemporary. But very little has been spoken or written about *our Lord* in this *mandate*.

This was the resurrected Lord, giving His last command. First, He was a *Visionary*. His words and thoughts centered around the *world:* Go into all the world. Today's Christian's responsibility is the world. All have the mandate to go to all corners of the world. Our Lord gave us no option.

Secondly, we are to preach the gospel. "Teach all nations, baptizing them." Our Lord expected results! Dr. Luke picked up this theme in Luke 19:10. Read it.

Thirdly, Christ shared the promise which guarantees victory: "Lo, I am with you alway, even unto the end of the world [age]." His com-

"And that, knowing the time, that now it is high time to awake out of sleep: for now is our salvation nearer than when we believed. The night is far spent, the day is at hand: let us therefore cast off the works of darkness, and let us put on the armour of light" (Rom. 13:11, 12).

mand ended with a positive note: "I am with you . . . unto the end." This is victory. Nothing is as good as His promised presence to a Church given a mandate by the greatest Visionary of all time.

Our Lord's mandate is repeated with a different emphasis on at least four different occasions following His resurrection. Thus the church will never get through its going, preaching, discipling and baptizing until the last sinner has been added to the Body of Christ.

This mandate should be our goal—doing what the Lord considered priority: missions, world evangelism.

II. The Church's Perspective

The growing Christian desires to know what is going on in the world. He places great importance on understanding the Scripture.

The most successful missionary of the first century, the Apostle Paul, wrote Romans 13:11, 12. Note his phrase, "Knowing the time." Paul was keenly aware of his Christian responsibility to spread the gospel; yet he knew that he was living during a specific time in history. Trends, moods, political structures and philosophies were leaving their tracks in time. Plato and Aristotle had preceded him. Persecution of the Church had already left this young Body scattered and scared.

We must be aware of the *now*. Carefully read the following facts regarding perspective.

A. Strategy Old But New

This is found in Acts 1:8. Read it. The order of this developed strategy is imperative in our practice. It begins at home (our Jerusalem) and extends outward to all corners of the world. There has never been a strong, effective foreign missionary outreach without a sound Biblical base at home. In establishing a beachhead for world evangelism, the operation begins where you are geographically. That is your Jerusalem.

B. The World Today

As early as five years ago, educators, diplomats and leading political figures began using new terminology with reference to this planet. They refer to various collections of nations with the nomenclature of first world, second world, third world and fourth world.

The first world is comprised mostly of the Western world, the industrial democracies.

The second world would be the nations comprising the Communist states. The third world refers to those countries located below the thirtieth parallel north and populated by black, brown and yellow races. These countries struggle against immeasurable odds toward the goal of development. These Africans, Asians and Latin Americans share a similar world view, believing that history has

111

been unkind to them and that they have been exploited by colonialistic and imperialistic ambitions of the affluent nations. They also feel that current world policy has politically arranged things so they cannot attain a just portion of the world's goods. Thus they preach that there is a widening gap between the rich and poor nations. These sentiments and convictions are voiced in the U.N.

The fourth world comprises these very poor nations and impoverished people who will never make it without outside help.

When the missionary speaks of the "mission field," usually he refers to the third world—countries where evangelism has been taking place by missionaries sent from the first and second worlds. When missionaries speak of the national church, they refer to the newer churches emerging out of the third world.

For example, there are over 300 independent Baptist churches in the Philippines—fully organized and totally indigenous. In Brazil new Baptist churches are being planted every month.

Very little, if any, evangelism is taking place in this fourth world.

Growing churches and concerned Christians know their world and their time. They are perceptive about trends and moods. They can cope with the responsibility of reaching this kind of world with Christ's gospel.

C. Statistics Speak

In order to further sharpen our focus, we list a few other salient facts about this world and missions today.

1. Only 5 percent of all missionaries labor

among two-thirds of the world population.

2. Over half of the world will live and die without the privilege of seeing a medical doctor.

3. Less than 6 percent of the world population lives in the United States.

4. Over 400 million people daily face hunger and starvation.

5. Over 90 percent of all available spiritual leadership ministers to less than 6 percent of the world's population.

6. Over 4 billion people live in this world. This will more than double in the next 25 years.

III. The Perplexing Problems

Satan's strategy against world evangelism has been apparent since the early days of the Church. You have the powerful demonstration of the Holy Spirit in Acts 1 and 2, while in Acts 3—6 there is Satan's powerful presence. Satan is mentioned only once in these stated chapters (Acts 5:3), but all testify that he was hindering the spread of the gospel. As soon as the Holy Spirit came to empower the Church for missionary outreach, Satan launched his relentless and staggering counterattack.

Acts 3—6 speaks of three satanic weapons that are still in his arsenal. They are (1) indescribable persecution and violence; (2) the subtle weapon of deceit, Acts 4:32—5:11; (3) his uncanny ability to preoccupy the Apostles with well-meaning peripheral responsibilities. Their priority tasks were prayer and preaching the Word. However, they evidently had become sidetracked by the growing social needs of providing food for the widows (Acts 6:1, 2).

One lesson is too brief to relate all the problems confronting the twentieth-century New Testament church. However, a few major ones must be briefly cited.

A. Syncretism

The *New Webster Encyclopedia Dictionary* defines syncretism as "the attempted blending of irreconcilable principles or parties, as in philosophy or religion." Second Corinthians 2:11 states that we are not ignorant of Satan's devices. Here is one which is on the move. It is an all-out effort by key political and religious leaders to blend together all major and minor religions. The proponents of this thought feel that religions, and especially Christianity, have been divisive, producing disharmony among the world's peoples. Already the pain of this horrible satanic disease has been experienced by many of the third-world nations in Africa.

B. Ecumenism

This movement seeks to unite all of Christendom (Protestant and Roman Catholics). It was born in 1910 from a missionary concern articulated by the Edinburgh Conference. Again we see Satan's work of deceit in trying to promote a counterattack on pure Biblical Christianity. The ecumenists, through the World Council of Churches, preach that if we all come together and forget our differences, we will have a great impact on world society. The contrary has been true since statistics prove that the merging of various so-called Christian denominations has resulted in a decline in their missionary forces. Interestingly enough, from 1938 to 1968 the most dramatic rise in missionary forces took place among

Bible-believing Baptist churches and among other groups not associated with the National Council of Churches or the World Council. Ofttimes the course which the nonaffiliates have taken has been to divide rather than unite. However, the World Council of Churches continues to preach unity among all Christendom and is a very powerful satanic weapon.

C. Secularism

Again Webster defines this as "supreme or exclusive attention to the affairs of this life." He goes on to define the secularist as "one who rejects every form of religious faith . . . and one who believes that education and other matters should be conducted without the introduction of a religious element." Sad but true, this ideology has even hit our evangelical churches. This is especially true as Satan leads God's people to focus the greater percentage of time on "this life." All over this country there is an increased pursuit toward "laying up treasure upon this earth." We need to be sobered by the words of Mark 4:19. (Read.) The evil one preoccupies us with good secular activity that keeps us from practicing the priorities of reaching the world.

D. Sleepiness

There was a problem with spiritual somnolence with the disciples and early Christians. This is why Paul cried out, "It is high time to awake out of sleep" (Rom. 13:11). It is easy for a Christian to fall asleep while the world is dying and going to Hell. It seems that Satan has a special cradle designed for Bible Christians. Psychologists tell us that one sleeps best when he is totally relaxed. Perhaps the

115

Devil's method of attack is through the subtle device of relaxing the Christian from his duties and responsibilities. Then it is easy to fall asleep without telling the world about Christ.

Today evidence abounds that we are plagued with laymen and leaders with little concern.

IV. The Church's Needs

The listing of a few may serve to provoke future meditation and discussion.

A. Hold fast to Biblical doctrine.

B. Reaffirm our stand that man cannot be saved except through acceptance of the Lord Jesus Christ (Acts 4:12).

C. All-out prayer for the calling of dedicated missionaries to go into all the world.

D. Sustained virile interest in missions shown by the church family and leadership.

E. Bringing missions and missionaries into Christian homes.

F. A goal-oriented program promoting missions in all departments of the church.

G. A continual program of preaching and teaching, placing emphasis on our world responsibility.

H. An all-out visitation, soul-winning program in your Jerusalem.

I. The constant vision of churches mothering other churches.

Let us share a few personal notes.

Much of present-day Christianity is surface. There is little that runs as deep as the Scripture. When it comes to holiness, world evangelism, etc., one could get the impression that we have entered the Hollywood marketplace and find ourselves playacting parts of Christianity. We play up love, joy, peace; preach justification by faith and even give a gospel invitation. We talk about separation from the world, although we are hearing it less. However, to be real our people must be reintroduced to the other side of the gospel: persecution, tribulation, suffering and shame. Many talk about living for Christ, but few mention dying with Christ. We are off on a binge in talking about inner self-fulfillment while Christ talked about self-denial. The crossbearing of Mark 8 is certainly a part of Christianity.

The contemporary Body of Jesus Christ must be willing to present both sides of the coin when it comes to commitment and cost. Both have always been present when true Bible-believing Baptist churches made their greatest inroads into the pagan world.

Prepare To Discuss Intelligently

1. What do we mean by the first, second, third and fourth worlds as they relate to missions?

2. What strategy for missions did Christ set forth in Acts 1:8? Is it apropos today?

3. How do the satanic weapons of Acts 3—6 still apply today?

4. Name some problems facing missions now.

5. Which of the church's needs does your church need most?

CHAPTER 13

Sunday Observance

by G. ARTHUR WOOLSEY, D.D., President of Spurgeon Baptist Bible College, Mulberry, FL

BIBLE PORTIONS TO READ: Acts 20:6-12; 1 Corinthians 16:1-4; Hebrews 10:19-25; Revelation 1:10

IS IT RIGHT TO BUY groceries on Sunday? Should a Christian attend Sunday baseball games? Is it permissible for a believer to spend his Sundays at the lake or the beach? Our Puritan forefathers would have given a prompt answer to each of these questions. In every instance the answer would have been a resounding NO! Were they Biblical in holding such strict views concerning Sunday? What are your convictions concerning the observance of Sunday? Can you defend your views?

For the sake of simplicity we have organized this discussion of the Sunday question under four headings: (1) The Jewish Sabbath, (2) early Christian observance of the first day of the week, (3) the idea of the Christian Sabbath, (4) practical observations on Sunday observance today.

I. The Jewish Sabbath (Exod. 20:8-11)

The first appearance of the Sabbath idea is found in Genesis 2:3.

The Sabbath makes its next appearance in the giving of the Law. God gave Moses two tablets of stone on which there were the Ten Commandments engraved by the finger of God (Exod. 31:18). The fourth of the Ten Commandments established the seventh day of the week as the Sabbath, a day of rest (Exod. 20:8-11). The Sabbath was given as a sign between God and the Israelites (Exod. 31:13). It commemorated their miraculous deliverance from Egypt (Deut. 5:12-15). Work was prohibited on the Sabbath. Those who profaned the Sabbath were to be put to death (Exod. 32:14).

By the time of Christ the Sabbath had become a matter of observing rabbinical traditions rather than of a weekly day of remembrance and thanksgiving. The "sabbath day's journey" (Acts 1:12) illustrates the kind of rabbinical embroidery upon the Law which prevailed in Christ's day. The Jew was permitted to travel two thousand cubits (approximately 3,000 feet) on the Sabbath Day. If one exceeded this limit, he was guilty of working on the Sabbath Day.

There were several confrontations between the Pharisees and Christ over the manner of Sabbath observance. The Pharisees rebuked Him because the disciples plucked some heads of wheat on the Sabbath Day (Matt. 12:1-8). In His reply Christ made a statement which deserves special attention: "For the Son of Man is Lord even of the sabbath day" (Matt. 12:8). Thus He asserted His complete authority over the Sabbath. Later Paul was to write, "For Christ is the end of the law for righteousness to every one that believeth" (Rom. 10:4). The law of the Sabbath is included in this sweeping assertion.

II. Early Christian Observance of the First Day of the Week (Acts 20:6, 7)

A. The First Christians Were Jews

These early believers continued to meet in the Temple and in homes. They assembled daily including the Sabbath Day (Acts 2:46). However, at least four forces would arise which would tend to separate Christians from the Temple and from the observance of Jewish customs including the Sabbath: (1) Jewish persecution of Christians, (2) the controversy concerning the circumcision of Gentile believers, (3) God's revelation concerning the distinctive character of the Church and (4) the great numerical increase of Gentile believers.

1. *The Jewish Persecution of Christians (Acts 4:1–8:4)*. The Jewish leaders who had plotted Christ's arrest were quick to respond to Christianity. When Stephen preached Christ in the synagogue, he was arrested, brought to trial and stoned to death. This event ignited the fires of persecution (Acts 8:1). The fury of the Jewish leaders

was so great that the Christians, with the exception of the Apostles, fled to various places in Judaea and Samaria. The bitterness of the Jews toward the Christians was often implacable. On several occasions Paul was forced to lead the little flock of believers out of the synagogue to another meeting place. He did so at Corinth (Acts 18:4-7) and at Ephesus (Acts 19:9).

2. *The Controversy Concerning Circumcision of Gentile Converts (Acts 15:1-31; Gal. 2:11-21).* The conversion of Gentile believers was questioned and contested by some of the Jerusalem believers who had been raised as strict Pharisees. When some of these brethren visited the Antioch church, they caused a great commotion. They insisted that the Gentiles in the church could not be saved unless they were first circumcised and thereby undertook the obligations of the Law of Moses. Here was an all-important issue. The Antioch church decided to send a delegation to the Apostles in Jerusalem for a ruling on the matter. The Apostles decided resoundingly against the circumcision of the Gentiles. Even Peter, rebuked by Paul in Antioch, took a strong stand for the principle of salvation by faith apart from the works of the Law. While the issue did not die in spite of the strong stand taken by the Apostles, the controversy drew sharp lines of distinction between Law and grace and between Judaism and Christianity.

3. *God's Revelation Concerning the Distinctive Character of the Church.* God's plans for the Church and the Age of Grace were revealed in Paul's epistles. The Church was a mystery, a part of God's plan which had not been previously re-

vealed (Eph. 3:1-10). The setting forth of the doctrine of the Church further distinguished between Christianity and Judaism and stimulated the movement of separation between them.

4. *The Great Numerical Growth of the Gentile Believers*. As Christianity spread, the number of Gentile converts increased remarkably. By the end of the first century Christianity was predominantly Gentile. Jerusalem had been destroyed in A.D. 70. The Jerusalem church was no longer the center of Christian testimony. John was directed to address the Book of the Revelation to seven predominantly Gentile churches in Asia Minor. The increasing number of Gentile believers combined with the lessening influence of the Jerusalem church to complete the break between church and synagogue.

B. The First Day of First-Day Worship

The first Biblical record of regular worship on the first day of the week appears in the Book of Acts (Acts 20:6, 7). Paul was revisiting the city of Troas. The believers had adopted the custom of meeting on the first day of the week. Not only did Paul *not* reprove them, but he joined with them in their service and preached his famous long sermon during which Eutychus fell asleep and tumbled from the third loft. Reference is made to the first day of the week in Paul's first letter to the Corinthians also (1 Cor. 16:2). John refers to the Lord's Day in Revelation 1:10.

C. Confirmed by the Church Fathers

The writings of the Church Fathers establish several important points: (1) It was the common

...ns to meet on the first day of
...rst day of the week was usually
...Day; (3) this day was celebrated
...er, commemorating Christ's res-
...4) it was a day of rejoicing. We
...each point.

...ddle of the second century Justin
...red worship on the first day of the
...first day of creation in Genesis. He
...el between "Let there be light" and
...of "the Sun of righteousness" (Mal.
...first day of the week.

...riter of *Didache* at the end of the first
...ke of believers "having met together
...l's Day, break bread and give thanks."

5. ...riter of the *Epistle of Barnabas* defends
the Christian practice of meeting on the first day of
the week on the grounds that it commemorates the
resurrection of Christ, His first appearance to His
disciples and His ascension. Augustine (A.D.
359—430) wrote: "Sabbath signifies rest; Sunday
signifies resurrection."

4. The third century Didascalia Apostolorum
stated: "On Sunday be always joyful for who is
afflicted on Sunday commits a sin." Tertullian
(A.D. 150—230) advocated abstention from un-
necessary work on the Lord's Day, not out of respect for the Old Testament Law but as an aid in
observing the day as a day of rejoicing.

III. The Idea of Sunday-Sabbath

The Sunday-Sabbath doctrine probably originated around A.D. 700. Alucin (A.D. 733) is thought
by some to be the father of the Sunday-Sabbath
concept. Charlemagne, the Frankish emperor, is-

sued a series of edicts in the early 800s establishing Sunday as God's Sabbath. The idea persisted and was reinforced by the decrees of various popes and councils.

The Reformers rejected the Sunday-Sabbath idea. Luther felt every day was essentially alike (Rom. 14:5). He said one day of the week should be set aside for religious purposes, and he saw no reason for making a change since Sunday was established. Calvin considered establishing Thursday as the day of worship.

It remained for the Puritans to seize upon the Sunday-Sabbath idea and to revive its popularity. Puritan Nicholas Bownde penned a treatise entitled *The Doctrine of the Sabbath* in the late 1500s. When the Puritans seized control of the English Parliament in 1640, they promptly passed stringent laws regulating Sabbath conduct. One section of their laws prohibited "vainly and profanely walking for pleasure." With the restoration of the monarchy the pendulum swung in the opposite direction. Trading was resumed on Sunday, and the theaters were reopened.

The Puritans had their greatest opportunity to enforce their Sabbath convictions in America. Sunday-Sabbath was observed in the original colonies. Sunday "blue laws" were established at an early date. The Revolution did not reverse this trend. While the Federal Constitution prohibited the establishment of religion, state after state adopted "blue laws." Soon every state in the Union except one had them.

Historians generally attribute the decline of Sabbatarianism in America to immigration. As America became the "melting pot" of the nations,

124

many immigrants came from cultures which did not include the strict observance of Sunday. The industrial revolution also contributed to the repeal of Sunday laws. As America became more and more industrialized and less agricultural, Sunday work became increasingly more common.

Sunday in America is no longer the Sabbath. It is not the Lord's Day. It is not even "church day" for most Americans. Perhaps Sunday today can best be described as "Recreation Day." To millions of Americans Sunday is "golf day," "football day," "racetrack day," "boating day" or "shopping day." Unfortunately numerous professing Christians are among these.

IV. Practical Observations Concerning Sunday Observance Today

We believe that there are powerful arguments in favor of observing Sunday as the Lord's Day.

1. The Apostle Paul joined in the first-day-of-the-week service at Troas and preached there. In this case, at least, there is apostolic sanction for Christian worship on Sunday.

2. Early Christians observed the first day of the week as the Lord's Day. In it they celebrated the resurrection of Christ.

3. Observing the Lord's Day provides a weekly time of rejoicing in Christ's resurrection.

4. Giving God one day out of seven acknowledges that all of our time belongs to God even as giving one tenth of our income recognizes that all of our money is His.

5. The Christian home is blessed by a "Lord's Day" atmosphere. The children will learn lasting lessons from the attitudes of their parents.

6. Church attendance is promoted where Sunday is the Lord's Day. We are commanded not to forsake the assembling of the saints (Heb. 10:25).

7. A good testimony will be given to neighbors who observe that Sunday is a special day to the Christian family.

8. Observance of the Lord's Day will give needed rest. In the giving of the Law, God provided one day of rest in seven. Rest is necessary for both body and mind. Even the Communists have discovered that body and mind break down if there are not periodic rest periods.

Prepare To Discuss Intelligently

1. What lessons can we learn by studying the Jewish Sabbath?

2. Why do we insist that Sunday is not the Sabbath?

3. Should Christians seek the reenactment of Sunday "blue laws"?

4. What practical steps may a believer take to make Sunday the Lord's Day in his life?